D1611554

Of Earth and Darkness

OF EARTH
AND DARKNESS

The Novels of
William Golding

Arnold Johnston

University of Missouri Press
Columbia & London
1980

Library of Congress Cataloging in Publication Data

Johnston, Arnold.
    Of earth and darkness.

    Bibliography: p. 118
    Includes index.
    1. Golding, William Gerald, 1911– —Criticism
and interpretation. I. Title.
    PR6013.O35Z688   823'.9'14   79–3332
    ISBN 0–8262–0292–6

Portions of chapter four appeared in *William Golding: Some Critical Considerations*, copyright © 1978 by the University Press of Kentucky, and are used here by permission of the publishers.

Portions of chapter seven appeared in *Critique: Studies of Modern Fiction* 14:2 (172): 97–112.

Selections from *Lord of the Flies* reprinted by permission of Coward, McCann & Geoghegan, Inc., from *Lord of the Flies* by William Golding. Copyright © 1954 by William Gerald Golding.

Selections from *The Inheritors* reprinted by permission of Harcourt Brace Jovanovich, Inc. Copyright © 1962.

Selections from *Pincher Martin* reprinted by permission of Harcourt Brace Jovanovich, Inc. Copyright © 1957.

Selections from *Free Fall* reprinted by permission of Harcourt Brace Jovanovich, Inc. Copyright © 1960.

Selections from *The Spire* reprinted by permission of Harcourt Brace Jovanovich, Inc. Copyright © 1964.

Selections from *Darkness Visible* reprinted with the permission of Farrar, Straus & Giroux, Inc., from *Darkness Visible* by William Golding. Copyright © 1979 by William Golding.

Selections from *Lord of the Flies*, *The Inheritors*, *The Spire* and *Darkness Visible* reprinted by permission of Faber and Faber Limited, holder of world rights exclusive of U.S.A.

For Kristin

Acknowledgments

I wish to acknowledge the following debts of gratitude: to the Department of English, Western Michigan University, for providing time to see this study through publication; to Dr. Sara Leopold, Professor of Humanities, Wayne State University, for first bringing me to the novels of William Golding and for pointing me toward a career in higher education; to Dr. Ronald E. Martin, Professor of English, University of Delaware, for advice and encouragement in the early stages of this project; to Dr. Edward Callan, Professor of English, Western Michigan University, for his always generous recognition of his younger colleagues; to my wife, Kristin, for her invaluable assistance in indexing this study and for her general selflessness; and to my parents, James R. and Eliza Johnston.

Introduction

The literary success of *Lord of the Flies* is today an established fact, and William Golding now occupies a secure place among the finest of his fellow novelists. However, when the book appeared in 1954 it was regarded by most reviewers merely as an exciting, if somewhat unpleasant, juvenile adventure story. And its author, a forty-three-year-old schoolmaster and wartime commander in the British Royal Navy, hardly fit the usual image of a novelist at the outset of a brilliant career. However, over the years *Lord of the Flies* sold steadily and with increasing momentum; notably, a great many of its readers were young people. As Lionel Trilling said: "First, apparently, in the colleges, then in the secondary schools, it seems to have captured the imagination of a whole generation."[1] So great became the popularity of the "new" book that it began (in a "conflict" now subsided) to challenge J. D. Salinger's *The Catcher in the Rye*, which since 1945 had been the favorite of young readers.

But Golding's book represented an attitude and a literary mode much different from that of Salinger. *The Catcher in the Rye*, capturing deftly in its first-person narrative the idiom and viewpoint of the American adolescent, is nothing if not contemporary. Holden Caulfield's story is satirical, but he is a boy struggling with the realization that he is alive in a world, a universe, that cares nothing for him and that he cannot change. Thus, in Salinger's novel, we have the picture of an innocent who falls victim to a guilty society. In *Lord of the Flies*, however, Golding seems to hark back to an older, darker moral viewpoint, narrowing guilt from that artificial construct called society to the individual human being. And from a literary standpoint, too, Golding seems on the face of it to bring his readers to grips with the past. *Lord of the Flies* is a modern version of R. M. Ballantyne's nineteenth-century juvenile novel, *The Coral Island*; but, as will be discussed later, Golding's literary mode here is reminiscent of a period far more remote than that of Ballantyne. Suffice it to say that *Lord of the Flies* has been read and discussed widely as the work of a literary maverick, a writer who dares to be didactic, and whose moral platform seems uncomfortably close—in these iconoclastic times—to the orthodox religious doctrine of Original Sin. Both points seem to be borne out by several of Golding's subsequent novels.

Although the preceding estimate of what Golding is about needs much qualification and amendment, it serves to indicate that he is one of the most dynamic, exciting, and controversial figures in contemporary British literature, highly praised by many critics for his virtuosity and moral intensity, and dismissed by others as a heavy-handed fabulist whose vision is at once derivative and eccentric.

Golding's creations are pervaded at once by a keen sense of history and by numerous direct and indirect responses to both the literary past and critical commentaries on his own work. James R. Baker, in his fine study, *William Golding*, points out some useful parallels and connections between Golding's work and the ancient Greeks, to whom Golding has several times acknowledged an artistic debt. And Bernard S. Oldsey and Stanley Weintraub, in *The Art of William Golding*, trace many—almost too many—similar debts to contemporary sources. But while these approaches are both illuminating and provocative, they are perhaps less important to an understanding of the tendencies in Golding's work than the direct evidence of his expanding concept of his craft, reflected in his technical experimentation, and of his changing vision, reflected in the growing thematic complexity of his works.

Like Mark Kinkead-Weekes and Ian Gregor in their excellent *William Golding, A Critical Study*, I have chosen to follow this last direction in organizing the present study of Golding. Such an examination shows Golding's movement from the probing of individual human guilt in the context of isolated groups (*Lord of the Flies*, *The Inheritors*), through a middle stage placing greater emphasis on the role of self (*Pincher Martin*, *Free Fall*, *The Spire*), to his current attempt to integrate the consideration of self and society into a broader, more conventional framework of human action and experience (*The Pyramid*, *Darkness Visible*).

Also evident from novel to novel is Golding's growing concern with both the aesthetic and ethical aspects of perceiving and communicating truth—in short, with the nature of his own art. And this concern leads him from a technical approach that in *Lord of the Flies* seems predominantly formal, in which characterization and action are relatively subservient to the novel's thematic content, to one that in *Darkness Visible* seems intent on creating among character, plot, and theme a balance more in keeping with novelistic conventions. Particularly notable from a technical standpoint are the poetic intensity of Golding's descriptive prose and his many experiments with the limited point of view, which often lead, as in *The Inheritors* and *Pincher Martin*, to works that are astonishing tours de force. Golding's career hardly reflects the conversion of an allegorist into a social novelist; but it does reflect the developing complexity of an essentially symbolic vision, with a concomitant increase in concern for the unity of form and substance.

Golding's use of other literary works as ironic parallels to his own, and his apparent requirement of a protagonist who is a foil to his own vision, is at once his most striking limitation and a major source of his unique power. When he chooses such literary parallels wisely, as in *Lord of the Flies* (Ballantyne's *Coral Island*) and *The Inheritors* (H. G. Wells's *Outline of History*), the novels demonstrate the comparative richness and complexity of Golding's vision; but when he chooses unwisely, as he may have done in *The Pyramid* (Dickens's *Great Expectations*), one is sharply conscious of his limitations, especially as a creator of complex character and plot. Similarly, when his protagonist is a foil from whom he is sufficiently detached, like Christopher Martin or Dean Jocelin, Golding's works attain their full dramatic power and intensity; but when, as with Sammy Mountjoy and Oliver, his own consciousness is too closely involved with that of his major character, the intensity of his work is vitiated, its dramatic power dissipated. The resolution of these related problems seems to be the major challenge that Golding meets triumphantly in his latest novel, *Darkness Visible*.

Although this study is concerned mainly with his novels, Golding has produced other works that, at the least, have provided illuminating insights into his major fiction. His first published effort was a collection of poetry, simply entitled *Poems*, that appeared in 1934 as part of Macmillan's Contemporary

Poets Series. The various critical uses to which this early literary
venture has been put since his rise to prominence has led Golding to remark: "I quite see that my furtive efforts to conceal,
destroy, and at any rate disclaim that melancholy slim volume of
my extreme youth are not going to work."[2] And despite the fact
that Golding's own harsh estimate of his book seems sound, one
may nevertheless see here and there within its covers hints of the
spirit that was later to find full expression in his novels. From a
scholarly standpoint, perhaps the most useful of Golding's "secondary" works is *The Hot Gates*, a collection of essays written
since his career as a novelist began, providing valuable information, both literary and biographical, that I shall allude to frequently in the following pages.

Since Golding continues to be productive, final judgment on
his status must be reserved. However, since his work to date has
been accompanied by a good deal of controversial, often superficial, criticism, at least a tentative examination seems desirable.
Besides the three book-length studies of Golding mentioned earlier, one may turn to several other books: two simply entitled
William Golding, one by Bernard F. Dick, the other by Leighton
Hodson; *The Novels of William Golding*, by Howard S. Babb;
and *William Golding: The Dark Fields of Discovery*, by Virginia
Tiger. The scholar will find, too, several other useful critical ad-
juncts: a casebook edition of *Lord of the Flies*, comprising text,
notes, and a number of critical essays, edited by James R. Baker
and Arthur P. Ziegler, Jr.; *William Golding's "Lord of the Flies,"
A Source Book*, edited by William Nelson, containing numerous
early (and frequently slight) reviews and articles, as well as a
section of readings "related" to *Lord of the Flies; William Golding*, a brief study by Samuel Hynes, written as part of the Columbia University Press Essays on Modern Writers series; a collection of essays entitled *A William Golding Miscellany* in
Georgia State College's Studies in the Literary Imagination; and
William Golding: Some Critical Considerations, edited by Jack
I. Biles and Robert O. Evans, a collection of essays that also
supplies the most complete bibliography to date. I hope that the
following chapters may prove to be in sum at least complemen-
tary to the growing body of serious and competent Golding criticism, and that they do a measure of justice to one of the few
genuinely exciting writers of our generation.

Contents

1.

Indices and Influences

In 1962, when William Golding was lecturing in the United States, he outlined the development of his philosophical attitude as follows:

> Before the second world war I believed in the perfectibility of social man; that a correct structure of society would produce goodwill; and that therefore you could remove all social ills by a reorganization of society. It is possible that today I believe something of the same again; but after the war I did not because I was unable to. I had discovered what one man could do to another. . . . I believed then, that man was sick—not exceptional man, but average man. I believed that the condition of man was to be a morally diseased creature and that the best job I could do at the time was to trace the connection between his diseased nature and the international mess he gets himself into.[1]

The tracing of that connection produced *Lord of the Flies*.

Although dramatically centered upon the events of World War II, Golding's shift from rationalism to the moral viewpoint that controlled his first novel—that continues to mold his work despite the cautious and partial disclaimer above—may be traced through a number of earlier influences.

Golding's father was a master at Marlborough Grammar School, where the writer himself was to be a pupil, and his influence on Golding seems to have been profound. "He was incarnate omniscience," writes Golding of his father:

> I have never met anybody who could do so much, was interested in so much, and who knew so much. He could carve a mantelpiece or a jewel box, explain the calculus and the ablative absolute. He wrote a textbook of geography, of physics, of chemistry, of botany and zoology, devised a course in astronavigation, played the violin, the 'cello, viola, piano, flute. He painted expertly, knew so much about flowers he denied me the simple pleasure of looking anything up for myself. He produced a cosmology which I should dearly love to pass off as

1

all my own work because he never told anyone but me about it. . . .
He inhabited a world of sanity and logic and fascination.[2]

Of the supremely, though gently, rational household headed by
his father, Golding asks: "How could I talk to them about darkness and the irrational?" (*The Hot Gates*, p. 170). The threat-
ening shadows of those days were merely the fears of childhood,
but Golding's reminiscences seem to indicate that even then he
was struck by the existence of primitive undercurrents in an otherwise enlightened and commonsensical world.

Golding's childhood retreat from the warring nature of this
world was a large chestnut tree, in whose branches "neither the
darkness of the churchyard nor the vast pattern of work and
career and importance could get at me" (p. 170). From here he
watched, unseen, the world below, catching from passersby brief
glimpses of, and allusions to, additional mysteries of life—like
sex—that his child's mind only vaguely apprehended. In reading
Golding's account of this episode, one recognizes the roots of
the tree in *The Inheritors* from which vantage point Lok and Fa
are similarly exposed to a new and mysterious knowledge of
man's nature.

Golding's first days at school were marked by his prophetically inordinate fascination with words (which he often made up
himself) and by—as he remembers it—his almost exclusive concern with himself. This self-preoccupation as a child impressed
Golding so much that he makes it the subject of one of his few
autobiographical essays, "Billy the Kid," and its pervasive influence in his fiction is obvious. Golding's experience with children
has been refreshed many times since his own childhood: as a
schoolmaster himself, and as a father, he has "lived for many
years with small boys," years that he believes have enabled him
to "understand and know them with awful precision" (p. 88).
Although I shall suggest in the following pages that perhaps his
knowledge seems at times too precise, clearly Golding's experiences as child and teacher have played a large part in determining both the content and tenor of his writing.

While a student at Brasenose College, Oxford, from 1930 until 1934, Golding studied science and literature and found himself formally exposed to the spirit of confident scientific humanism that had characterized his father's world. Even then,
however, when his own rationalism was presumably at its

2

strongest, and when his writing, too, as in his early poems, was self-consciously literary and academic, Golding evinced occasional skepticism. Perhaps prompted by childhood memories of "darkness and the irrational," several of his "Oxford poems" question, as James Baker puts it, "the neat rationalism of the scientists and historians he was reading at the time."[3]

Among these poems is the satirical "Mr. Pope," in which Alexander Pope, a major apostle of the well-ordered universe, complains to God that "the stars are rather out of hand," and points out that

"If they would dance a minuet
Instead of roaming wild and free
Or stand in rows all trim and neat
How exquisite the sky would be!"   (*Poems*, p. 26)

And in "Vignette," Golding again undercuts the frequent narrow-mindedness of commonsensical man, while at the same time showing a healthy skepticism toward his equally limited, if more dynamic, counterpart:

Demos, ruddy, round, and short,
Made bolder by the inky port,
With slobbered mouth and frantic eyes,
Urges revolt and "Onward!" cries,
"The barricades!"
                                But still the squire,
Didactic by the flapping fire,
Puts back the ticking clock of heaven
And keeps the world at half-past seven.   (p. 13)

These two brief glimpses of his first published work—while giving some indication of the reason for Golding's obvious discomfort at their existence in print—show at least a tendency toward the pattern of thought that informs his novels, and show his maturing apprehension of the truth in his then callow-sounding "Song of the Flowers at Land's End": "It must remain/Most sweet and terrible to live" (p. 21).

Golding's poetry, moreover, was not the only symptom of his drift away from rationalism. Upon entering Oxford he had intended to major in science, but after two years he decided that science was not for him and turned to English literature, particularly that of the Anglo-Saxon period. Of this schism in Golding's education Bernard Oldsey and Stanley Weintraub have observed: "What have remained apparent in his writing are his academically split personality, his science-versus-the-humanities point of view, and the habit of running literary experiments which still smack of the laboratory he rejected."[4] Golding himself apparently discovered during the switch what he calls one of the major influences on his own work, the anonymous Old English epic fragment *The Battle of Maldon*.[5] One suspects upon reading this piece—a grim but heroic account of English defeat at the hands of invading Danes—that Golding may have been pulling the legs of would-be source hunters, although the austere poetry and pessimistic tone of the dour tale bear resemblance at least in spirit to Golding's own prose.

Golding's interest in literature was hardly new. From his initial fascination with words he had gone on to read avidly both children's literature and the major British writers, and, since his days at Marlborough Grammar School, he had been reading the ancient Greeks. Baker asserts that "the Greeks, taken collectively, represent one of the most potent forces in shaping (or confirming) Golding's conception of human psychology and human fate."[6] As with *Maldon*, I believe that the influence of the Greeks is, on the whole, more pervasive than specific. But there is little doubt that Baker's point is well-taken; and, indeed, he does suggest specific relationships between *Lord of the Flies* and *The Bacchae* of Euripides that can scarcely be coincidental.[7]

After his graduation from Oxford and the publication of his *Poems*, Golding was involved for a time in writing, acting, and producing for, as Oldsey and Weintraub put it, "a small non-West End London theater,"[8] experiences he obviously made use of in writing *Pincher Martin*. In 1939 he married and began teaching at Bishop Wordsworth's School in Salisbury. Then came the war, during which Golding served from 1939 to 1945 in the Royal Navy, encountering directly the brutalities of combat, and indirectly "the vileness beyond all words that went on, year after year, in the totalitarian states" (*The Hot Gates*, pp. 86–87). These experiences sickened him and strikingly confirmed the view of man and the impetus to communicate it that engendered *Lord of the Flies*.

Golding returned from the war to teach again at Bishop

Wordsworth's, and to write. One sees, however, since *Lord of the Flies* was not published until 1954, that it was hardly written in a white-hot fervor at the close of the war. Indeed, *Lord of the Flies* was written only after several other novels had been rejected by publishers and presumably discarded by their author, and was itself rejected by no less than twenty-one publishers before its acceptance by Faber and Faber.[9]

Thus, the excerpt from Golding's 1962 lecture, quoted at the beginning of this chapter, is seen to be somewhat misleading in that the form, style, and content—as well as the philosophical viewpoint—of his first novel were in large part determined by many prewar influences and experiences that Golding probably turned to gradually as his initial failures refined his gifts and caused him to look for ways to suggest the links between man's vividly etched present and his enduring past.

I have already pointed to several incidents from Golding's life that seem to have found their way into his novels, and I shall have more to say about these and other such biographical parallels in the following chapters. One can do little more than conjecture about the nature of the discarded manuscripts, but it seems clear that part of Golding's evolution as a writer during those nine years after the war involved his learning how to utilize most effectively not only the ideas and techniques of other writers, but also the facts of his own life that provided him with the only firsthand empirical data by which to test his views of human nature.

Perhaps the area in which Golding most strikingly shows the influences of his early reading and his years at Oxford is that of form. John Peter, in one of the few useful early articles on Golding, called the novelist's works "fables" rather than "fictions," defining "fables" as: "those narratives which leave the impression that their purpose was anterior, some initial thesis or contention which they are apparently concerned to embody and express in concrete terms." Peter's main criticism of Golding's work—with particular reference to *Lord of the Flies*—is based upon his view of Golding as a fabulist: "The fault is precisely that which any fable is likely to incur: the incomplete translation of its thesis into its story so that much remains external and extrinsic, the teller's assertion rather than the tale's enactment before our eyes."[10]

5

Disputing Peter's classification of Golding—again primarily with reference to his first novel—Ian Gregor and Mark Kinkead-Weekes argue in the introduction to their "School Edition" of *Lord of the Flies* that the book is "a fable and a fiction *simultaneously*," since it does not merely assert an abstract proposition, but creates a vivid fictional world that *shows* rather than *tells* us the truth as Golding sees it.[11] Gregor and Kinkead-Weekes, however, seem here to disagree less with Peter's classification than with his judgment of Golding's success in "embodying or expressing his fable in concrete terms," and in their full-length study of Golding's novels they recant somewhat, describing his work as progressing from "fable . . . gradually assumed into myth located in history."[12] In any case, Golding himself liked Peter's article, and his 1962 lecture (appropriately entitled "Fable") is largely an attempt to explain his adopted role as fabulist. He did qualify his endorsement of Peter's term in a 1959 interview with Frank Kermode:

> Well, what I would regard as a tremendous compliment to myself would be if someone would substitute the word "myth" for "fable" because I think a myth is a much profounder and more significant thing than a fable. I do feel fable as being an invented thing on the surface whereas myth is something which comes out from the roots of things in the ancient sense of being the key to existence, the whole meaning of life, and experience as a whole.[13]

Here, however, Golding is hardly arguing with Peter's main contention that his novels seem to be embodiments of previously formulated theses, a point that one may confirm merely by reference to the quotation at the beginning of this chapter. And despite the fact that even his early novels do function more nearly within the complex archetypal and spiritual scope of myth than the simple and morally aphoristic confines of fable, their major technical flaw seems precisely to be the didacticism that Peter has noted. This aspect of his work has been a major source of concern for Golding, and from novel to novel one may trace his attempts to break free from the tendency to reduce life to pattern.

At all events, one readily sees that Golding's formal approach to the novel shows the marks of his early interest in ancient literature, both Greek and Anglo-Saxon, even in a list of such general characteristics of his fiction as the following: 1) his desire to be seen as a "maker of myths"; 2) his general reliance on simple situations and plots that either partake of or suggest mythical archetypes; 3) his concern in making his novels the concrete expressions of spiritual or moral assumptions; 4) his suggestion of an inevitability in human actions akin to the ancient concept of Fate; 5) his primary use of the process of gradual self-discovery as a plot device; 6) his use of irony as a major narrative technique. With reference to point two, even his use of contemporary sources may be seen as a way of giving a sense of archetypal continuity between the complex, interwoven structure of ancient myth and the "myths" of the present. In her 1974 study, Virginia Tiger calls Golding's narrative technique "ideographic," and makes a thorough and valuable analysis of the way in which Golding offers two major thematic perspectives in each novel.[14]

Another of Golding's early interests, the influence of which may be seen most clearly in *Free Fall* and *The Pyramid*, is Egyptology. This fascination with a culture so different from that of Greece seems to play a considerable part in the most recent developments in Golding's fiction, and perhaps may indicate the spirit of changes yet to come.

All of Golding's novels, from *Lord of the Flies* to *Darkness Visible*, show in one way or another his preoccupation with the points discussed above. In the following chapters I shall explore more fully all of the matters touched upon by this introductory discussion. I shall attempt to show, too, those facets of Golding's fiction that mark him as a writer of great skill and originality, and not merely a derivative product of previous literary influences and traditions.

2.

Lord of the Flies:
Fable, Myth, and Fiction

Lord of the Flies deals, ostensibly, with a group of English schoolboys who, in the process of being evacuated by airplane from the dangers of a nuclear war, find themselves alone on a tropical island after their plane crashes. The boys, ranging in age from about six to thirteen, are faced with the problem of survival on the uninhabited island while attempting to attract the attention of passing ships and planes.

The problem of physical existence solves itself—the island is rich in fruit and game and the climate is favorable. The real problem that arises among the boys involves their own inner nature, and emerges most directly from a clash between those who wish to keep a fire burning on the island's mountain to attract rescuers and those who wish to hunt and indulge in what at first seems to be the natural inclination of children toward unrestrained play. The conflict begins in apparent childish innocence, and reaches its climax in acts of shocking brutality that carry far-reaching implications of guilt.

Golding has summed up the theme of *Lord of the Flies* as follows:

> The theme is an attempt to trace the defects of society back to the defects of human nature. The moral is that the shape of society must depend on the ethical nature of the individual and not on any political system however apparently logical or respectable. The whole book is symbolic in nature.[1]

As I have mentioned, Golding feels that evil arises from man's essential being, and he attempts to demonstrate his thesis in this self-consciously symbolic work which shows civilization totally unable to contend with man's apparently natural and voracious propensity for savagery. A systematic probing into the question of man's inherent good or evil is, without doubt, one of Golding's major concerns; and in the course of this study I shall attempt to show that his apparent preoccupation with the problems of survival (*Lord of the Flies, The Inheritors, Pincher Martin*) is an important key to understanding both his philosophy and his techniques.

Lord of the Flies falls into that hardy genre of accounts of shipwreck and survival on tropical islands: *Robinson Crusoe, The Swiss Family Robinson, The Coral Island*, and so forth. Golding particularly wishes the reader to associate his novel with Ballantyne's *The Coral Island*. The two main characters in both books are named Ralph and Jack, and the relationship between the names of Ballantyne's Peterkin and Golding's Simon needs little elaboration. Then, too, there are two direct references to *The Coral Island* in Golding's book, one near the beginning—

> "It's like in a book."
> At once there was a clamour.
> "Treasure Island—"
> "Swallows and Amazons—"
> "Coral Island—"

and one near the end—

> The officer nodded helpfully.
> "I know. Jolly good show. Like the Coral Island."[2]

Frank Kermode and Carl Niemeyer, in separate essays, discuss at some length Golding's use of *The Coral Island* as an ironic parallel to his own novel, pointing out the difference between Golding's vision of human nature and what Niemeyer calls the "cheerful unrealities" of Ballantyne.[3] And Golding himself, in the interview with Kermode, had this to say of his book's connection with *The Coral Island*:

> What I'm saying to myself is, "Don't be such a fool, you remember when you were a boy, a small boy, how you lived on that island with Ralph and Jack and Peterkin. . . . Now you are grown up, . . . you can see people are not like that; they would not behave like that if they were God-fearing English gentlemen, and they went to an island like that." Their savagery would not be found in natives on an island.

9

As like as not they would find savages who were kindly and uncomplicated and that the devil would rise out of the intellectual complications of the three white men on the island itself.[4]

Golding's remark about kindly, uncomplicated savages stacks the anthropological cards a bit heavily against civilized man, and ignores a number of basic facts about primitive cultures. Of course, *Lord of the Flies* doesn't allow the reader any "real" savages with whom to compare the boys, as Golding's artistic sense evidently told him to avoid confusing the central human issue with such anthropological quibbles. However, the aforementioned remark does underline Golding's moralistic bias, and points toward a more serious charge that might be leveled against the novel: that his authorial presence is often overly obtrusive, either in didactic interpositions or, more seriously, in unconvincing manipulation of his characters.

In this connection Lionel Trilling says that Golding succeeds in persuading the reader that the boys' actions result from the fact that they "are not finally under the control of previous social habit or convention," but adds that he "should not have credited this quite so readily of American boys who would not . . . have been so quick to forget their social and moral pasts."[5] For my part, I am unable to see why Mr. Trilling is unwilling to carry his pertinent critical comment to its logical conclusion, without involving himself in speculations about the relative acculturation processes in Britain and the United States. Had he pursued his doubts to an expression of dissatisfaction with the credibility of the boys, he would have been on firmer ground, since there are several points at which Golding's manipulations of narrative and dialogue do ring false.

Two interrelated but discernibly distinct threads are evident in *Lord of the Flies*. One is the actual narrative, detailing meticulously the boys' descent into savagery; the other is the gradually developed symbol of the "Beast" that is first suggested by the wholly natural night fears of the "littluns" and that eventually becomes the object of worship by the boys-turned-savages. The Beast is an externalization of the inner darkness in the children's (man's) nature, and its ascendancy is steady, inexorable, as is the path to savagery, increasing in intensity with each new regression on the part of the boys. But despite his often brilliant handling of this apposite motivating symbol of the book, it is especially during scenes involving the Beast that Golding becomes particularly intrusive.

At one point, for instance, when the assembled boys are discussing the problem of the Beast, Piggy (the pragmatic rationalist) explains: "'Course there isn't a beast in the forest. How could there be? What would a beast eat?'" (p. 77). And the answer, supplied by the chorus of boys, is "'Pig!'"—to which the unmistakable voice of Golding (by way of reminding the reader just what his symbol represents) can be heard to add, "'We eat pig'" (p. 77). And a few pages later Simon, the convulsion-afflicted mystic, says of the Beast: "'What I mean is . . . maybe it's only us'" (p. 82). This rather subtle interpretation of human nature from a small boy demonstrates further that Golding is so intent on his moral message that he will not hesitate to make the youngsters dance to his tune.

This assembly scene is central to the novel's development in that it marks the last point at which "civilized" rules and procedures can be said to dominate the boys' words and actions. Grounds for the breakdown of the rules are furnished by dissent among the representatives of order (Ralph, Piggy, and Simon), as Piggy, with his unimaginative rationalist's intelligence, answers Simon's observation with a resounding "'Nuts!'" Even among the "civilized," communication is lacking, and when Jack—leader of the forces of disorder—shouts "'Bollocks to the rules!'" chaos and darkness are ushered in (p. 84).

However, Golding cannot let the matter of the Beast rest here, and after the assembly has dispersed, Ralph, shaken, turns to Piggy and asks, "'Are there ghosts, Piggy? Or Beasts?'" And here the ventriloquist's lips can be seen to move, as Piggy answers: "'Course there aren't. . . . 'Cos things wouldn't make sense. Houses an' streets, an'—TV—they wouldn't work'" (p. 85). Although beautifully camouflaged in boyish diction, the implication that a boy of about ten can reason that the existence of supernatural phenomena challenges the validity of natural law is simply too much to swallow.

A major objectification of man's inner Beast appears in the shape of a pig's head on a stick that Jack and his "hunters" leave as an offering for the Beast. Unknown to the hunters, Simon has been nearby during the killing of the pig, having hidden himself in some bushes at the onset of one of his fits. He is then left alone with the head, thus setting the scene for the most self-consciously symbolic incident in the book. At this point the significance of the book's title becomes evident, as the head, swarming with flies, enters into an imaginary conversation with Simon, a conversation in which Golding, speaking through this grotesque agent, removes any doubts that might still have lingered in the reader's mind with respect to the novel's theme or the source of the evil described therein:

> The Lord of the Flies spoke in the voice of a schoolmaster.
> "This has gone quite far enough. My poor, misguided child, do you think you know better than I do?"
> There was a pause.
> "I'm warning you. I'm going to get waxy. D'you see. You're not wanted. Understand? We are going to have fun on this island! So don't try it on, my poor misguided boy, or else—"
> Simon found he was looking into a vast mouth. There was blackness within, a blackness that spread.
> "—Or else," said the Lord of the Flies, "we shall do you. See? Jack and Roger and Maurice and Robert and Bill and Piggy and Ralph. Do you. See?"   (p. 133)

The above scene, which places perhaps the greatest strain on the reader's credulity, may be defended as the book's clearest indication that human guilt is pervasive, including even the "good" characters, Ralph and Piggy. However, by comparing this strained encounter between Simon and the head with the scenes immediately preceding and following it, one may see that Golding makes his point there just as clearly and much more effectively.[6]

The killing of the pig by Jack's hunters is a case in point. The pig-hunting of former days has been relatively innocent, but to fully dramatize the deep inner evil that takes possession of the boys after they accept the Beast as their god, Golding depicts more than a mere killing. Conjuring up the most shocking imagery he could use to show the degeneration of these preadolescents, he describes the slaughter of a mother sow in terms of a sexual assault.[7] How better to portray the children's loss of innocence (since children are no strangers to killing) than by picturing them as perpetrators of an Oedipal violation?

> . . . the sow staggered her way ahead of them, bleeding and mad, and the hunters followed, wedded to her in lust, excited by the long chase and the dropped blood. . . .

> Here, struck down by the heat, the sow fell and the hunters hurled themselves at her. This dreadful eruption from an unknown world made her frantic; she squealed and bucked and the air was full of sweat and noise and blood and terror. Roger ran round the heap, prodding with his spear wherever pigflesh appeared. Jack was on top of the sow, stabbing downward with his knife. Roger found a lodgment for his spear and began to push till he was leaning with his whole weight. The spear moved forward inch by inch and the terrified squealing became a high-pitched scream. Then Jack found the throat and the hot blood spouted over his hands. The sow collapsed under them and they were heavy and fulfilled upon her.   (p. 125)

The vividness of this scene makes it both a powerfully realistic component of the essential story and a major contribution to the novel's symbolic scheme. The episode involving Simon and the head, however—especially the "conversation"—is difficult to view in other than symbolic terms, marking it as another nagging flaw in a book that—whatever its thematic concerns—seems committed from the outset to creating believable boys on a believable island. Actually, the mere physical presence of the pig's head, the Lord of the Flies, would have served well without the didactic pronouncements, since "lord of the flies" is a translation of the Hebrew *Ba'al zevuv* (Beelzebub in Greek), implying quite effectively that the head is representative of man's "inner devil."

In any event, the most successful symbolic portrayal of the Beast as man appears earlier in the novel in the form of a dead airman whose parachute carries him in the night to the top of the mountain, where, tangled in the complication of strings, he becomes lodged in a sitting position, the upper half of his body alternately rising and falling as the breeze tightens and slackens the lines. Sam and Eric, the twins, are horrified by this grisly figure when they come to tend the fire, and when a subsequent expedition (headed by Ralph and Jack, but notably excluding Simon and Piggy) climbs the mountain to confirm the twins' garbled report, the following powerful passage shows the Beast impressed forever on the minds and hearts of the boys:

> Behind them the sliver of moon had drawn clear of the horizon. Before them, something like a great ape was sitting asleep with its head between its knees. Then the wind roared in the forest, there was confusion in the darkness and the creature lifted its head, holding toward them the ruin of a face.   (p. 114)

Of Earth and Darkness

This is the experience that accelerates the deterioration of civilized procedures, bringing confusion to the final assembly and committing Jack fully—in a parody of his initial appearance as leader of the choir, or perhaps an oblique commentary on the ritualistic mind—to high priesthood in the dark new religion. And it is to determine the truth of this experience and the nature of the so-called Beast from Air that Simon, after his ghastly interview with the head, courageously ascends the mountain, where he frees the wasted body "from the wind's indignity" (p. 135).

Simon, whom Golding has called quite explicitly a "Christ-figure," comes down from the mountain to carry the truth to the others, but—still weak from his recent attack—he stumbles instead into a ritual reenactment of the pig-killing and is killed by the frenzied and fear-maddened boys, who ironically mistake him for the Beast.[8] And here Golding's sweeping indictment of humanity becomes most nearly complete, for Ralph and Piggy, lured by the prospect of food, have temporarily joined with the hunters and take part, albeit unwittingly, in the murder of Simon. And here, too, at the moment of Simon's death, in the midst of a storm that thunders within as well as around them, the boys are visited by the spectre of human history, embodied in the form of the dead airman. Dislodged from atop the mountain and carried again into the air by the winds, the grotesque figure of the decaying parachutist plummets to the sands, scattering the terror-stricken boys, and sweeps far out to sea. The beach is left desolate save for the small broken body of Simon, which follows the parachutist into the sea:

> Along the shoreward edge of the shallows the advancing clearness was full of strange, moonbeam-bodied creatures with fiery eyes. Here and there a larger pebble clung to its own air and was covered with a coat of pearls. The tide swelled in and over the rain-pitted sand and smoothed everything with a layer of silver. Now it touched the first of the stains that seeped from the broken body and the creatures made a moving patch of light as they gathered at the edge. The water rose farther and dressed Simon's coarse hair with brightness. The line of his cheek silvered and the turn of his shoulder became sculptured marble. The strange attendant creatures, with their fiery eyes and trailing vapors, busied themselves round his head. The body lifted a fraction of an inch from the sand and a bubble of air escaped from the mouth with a wet plop. Then it turned gently in the water.
>
> Somewhere over the darkened curve of the world the sun and

14

moon were pulling, and the film of water on the earth planet was held, bulging slightly on one side while the solid core turned. The great wave of the tide moved farther along the island and the water lifted. Softly, surrounded by a fringe of inquisitive bright creatures, itself a silver shape beneath the steadfast constellations, Simon's dead body moved out toward the open sea.   (p. 142)

The amount and kind of description devoted to Simon's death is ample indication of his saintly role even without Golding's identification of him as a Christ-figure.

All of the obvious parallels to Christ are there—from Gethsemane to Golgotha—and one may easily identify Simon's story with that of many a martyred mystic.[9] But why are they there? Why is Simon there? Is Golding merely speaking with the voice of moral and religious orthodoxy? As his subsequent novels have shown, Golding is not to be labeled so easily. But in those novels one sees a consistent preoccupation with the artist or artist-figure, someone actively engaged in interpreting the human condition: Tuami, the tribal artist in *The Inheritors*; Christopher "Pincher" Martin, the penultimate actor in *Pincher Martin*; Sammy Mountjoy, the guilt-torn painter in *Free Fall*; Dean Jocelin and Roger Mason, creative force behind, and architect of, *The Spire*; Oliver, the confused would-be musician in *The Pyramid*; and Matty Windrove, the naive prophet of *Darkness Visible*.

Viewed in this light, Simon's habitual isolation from the other boys, his obvious inability to communicate to them the "truths" that he grasps intuitively, and finally his death at their hands, reflect the all-too-frequent fate of the artist in society. Of course, all that can be said of the artist's role may be applied to that of the religious or mystic; but again and again in his later works, Golding demonstrates that the nature of his unorthodoxy is its basis in that highly eclectic form of mysticism called art. Like many artists before him, he sees the artist as priest, as interpreter of life's mysteries and possible savior of mankind. Unlike many of his predecessors, though, Golding faces squarely the historical fact that the artist—like other saviors—has met with little success. And in this first novel, Simon should be recognized as the first of Golding's "portraits of the artist," embodying both his pride in the high calling and his frustration at the artist's inability to defend himself against the weaknesses of others, or to

15

transcend his own human frailties. Even more important to a reading of his works as a whole is the realization that, for Golding, the artist is representative of humanity at large, and that Golding finds in creativity the source of man's strength and weakness, his good and evil.

In any case, the aftermath of Simon's death is the last point at which *Lord of the Flies* can be said to picture the existence of a calm and ordering vision. Total disintegration of the civilized forces follows swiftly, beginning with the theft of Piggy's glasses—the source of fire and symbol of intellectual power—by Jack and his hunters, and proceeding through Piggy's murder by the brutal Roger to the final hunt for Ralph, who is to be decapitated and sacrificed like a pig to the Beast.

The description of Piggy's death provides an informing contrast to that of Simon's, showing quite clearly, though subtly, Golding's antirationalist bias:

> The rock struck Piggy a glancing blow from chin to knee; the conch exploded into a thousand white fragments and ceased to exist. Piggy, saying nothing, with no time for even a grunt, traveled through the air sideways from the rock, turning over as he went. The rock bounded twice and was lost in the forest. Piggy fell forty feet and landed on his back across that square red rock in the sea. His head opened and stuff came out and turned red. Piggy's arms and legs twitched a bit, like a pig's after it has been killed. Then the sea breathed again in a long, slow sigh, the water boiled white and pink over the rock; and when it went, sucking back again, the body of Piggy was gone.   (p. 167)

One notes here the same studious reportage of physical fact as in the passage quoted earlier. But this time Golding concentrates on matter-of-fact particulars, eschewing the angle of vision that might place Piggy's death in universal perspective: whereas Simon is described in language befitting a dead saint, Piggy is pictured as a dead animal. Of course, Piggy's actions immediately before his murder are brave in conventional terms; but his rationalist's faith in order and human perfectibility, ironically undercut throughout the book, seems nowhere more misguided than in this scene (p. 166). The mystic's intuitive recognition that good and evil coexist within man is the spark of his divinity; but the rationalist's denial of such intangible forces chains him forever to the material world of earth and organism.

16

After Piggy's death, Ralph finds himself being hunted by the other boys. But at the book's climactic moment, just as the "savages" are about to descend on Ralph, a "rescuer" appears in the person of a British naval officer. And at once, in a passage laden with irony, the shrieking painted savages become "a semicircle of little boys, their bodies streaked with colored clay, sharp sticks in their hands . . . standing on the beach making no noise at all" (p. 185). The officer, confronted with this scene of filth and disorder, rebukes the boys lamely (as Lionel Trilling might have noted): "'I should have thought that a pack of British boys—you're all British, aren't you?—would have been able to put up a better show than that—'" (p. 186). And Ralph, the book's Everyman, representative of the world of "longing and baffled common-sense" (p. 65), is left to weep "for the end of innocence, the darkness of man's heart, and the fall through the air of the true, wise friend called Piggy" (pp. 186–87).

Several early critics and reviewers of *Lord of the Flies* assailed the book's ending as too neat, if not actually as a question-begging compromise with lovers of happy endings.[10] However, a reflective reading shows that the "rescue" is no rescue at all: throughout the novel Golding is at pains to point out that the major human predicament is internal; the officer solves Ralph's immediate problem, but "the darkness of man's heart" persists. Practically, of course, as Golding says, in a book "originally conceived . . . as the change from innocence—which is the ignorance of self—to a tragic knowledge . . . If I'd gone on to the death of Ralph, Ralph would never have had time to understand what had happened to him."[11] And on a more sophisticated thematic level he observes, "The officer, having interrupted a man-hunt, prepares to take the children off the island in a cruiser which will presently be hunting its enemy in the same implacable way. And who will rescue the adult and his cruiser?"[12]

Returning to the Simon-Piggy contrast discussed earlier, one might also note that it is Piggy, the misguided rationalist, for whom Ralph sorrows, not Simon, the "saint." Besides subtly underscoring Golding's concern for the fate of the artist-mystic, this fact seems to indicate that Ralph's tragic experience has not finally brought him to the sort of self-knowledge that can save him as a man.[13] The implications for humanity at large are clear

17

and unencouraging. Thus, although the officer seems to suggest a deus ex machina, one will be hard pressed to find a happy ending here.

On a broader front, the plot of *Lord of the Flies* has been attacked as both eccentric and specious, either too far removed from the real world or too neatly microcosmic to be true.[14] The first of these charges, that of eccentricity, may be put aside for the time being. After all, removing one's setting and characters from the larger sphere of civilization has long been an acceptable, if not honorable, practice in almost every literary genre and tradition, as witness the success of Melville and Conrad, whose isolated fictional worlds remain real in both their concrete details and their human significance. The source of the objection seems to be predisposed literary tastes, rather than more rigorous aesthetic standards—preference for the novel as typical history, rather than symbolic vision. However, the related charge—that Golding oversimplifies complex truth through manipulation of his microcosmic world—is on firmer ground. And in speaking to this point, one must necessarily return to John Peter's identification of Golding as a fabulist, as well as to Golding's own wish to be seen as a "myth-maker."

The main concern, then, of both opponents and supporters of *Lord of the Flies* is whether or not it functions adequately on its primary, or "fictional," level; or more simply, is the story told convincingly? Peter, in "The Fables of William Golding," assails the novel for its "incomplete translation of its thesis into its story so that much remains external and extrinsic, the teller's assertion rather than the tale's enactment before our eyes." And indeed, I have detailed several instances of such didactic obtrusions, including some aspects of character and action that seem more concerned with theme than credibility. However, I would qualify Peter's observation rather strongly, noting that such instances seem more vulnerable to the charge of being extraneous than of betraying Golding's "incomplete translation" of his thesis, which is more than adequately communicated by the rest of the novel.

And what of the rest of the novel? Is it merely a skeleton of thesis incompletely fleshed by concrete detail? Kinkead-Weekes and Gregor are highly emphatic in answering this question: "Physical realities come first for Golding and should stay first for his readers."[15] They devote a long first chapter in their study to a demonstration of the "complex physical truth" of *Lord of the Flies*, concentrating heavily on the naturalistic clarity and inclusiveness of Golding's description, and arguing that his symbolic representations are often so reflective of life's complexities as to be actually ambiguous, perhaps even too ambiguous to be seen symbolically at all. This latter point is a bit extreme: Golding's main symbolic intentions are clear enough in the novel, even without the many explicit comments he has made since its publication. However, Kinkead-Weekes and Gregor may be excused their overstatement, since so much attention has been paid to the novel's symbolism that its objective vehicles have been too often deemphasized, if not forgotten.

And here, Golding's style becomes a major concern. As Kinkead-Weekes and Gregor demonstrate, Golding's descriptive prose carries the burden of his meaning and—coupled with the inexorable narrative of the boys' descent into chaos—provides the reader with a naturalistically concrete and complex surface world against which to view the symbolic drama. One need only note passages already quoted—the killing of the sow, the deaths of Simon and Piggy—to be convinced that the realities of *Lord of the Flies* live in the flesh, as well as in the abstract, comprising a universe not oversimplified, but paradoxically diverse, in which beauty and ugliness, good and evil, precariously coexist. The main features of Golding's best description are scientific accuracy and objectivity, combined with a felicitous use of simple adjectives and verbs that can transform his tersely pictured scenes into powerful evocations of transcendent beauty or obsessive ugliness. One thinks here of the extremes of such effects before the sow-killing, when "she staggered into an open space where bright flowers grew and butterflies danced round each other and the air was hot and still" (p. 125), and after, when "the pile of guts was a black blob of flies that buzzed like a saw" (p. 128). Without doubt, Golding's world exists compellingly on its primary level: its strained moments seem more like surface blemishes than structural defects, blemishes that catch the eye because of their dissimilarity to the skillfully woven fabric of the whole.

As for Golding's stature as a maker of myth, one must grant him a considerable measure of success. Certainly, if myth "comes out from the roots of things" and evokes age-old and recurrent human patterns, *Lord of the Flies* is much closer to myth than to simple fable. One may trace its literary roots alone back through the more immediate past (*The Coral Island*), to the ancient past (*The Bacchae*), and on a broader plane one may easily see in the story echoes and parallels from both the political and social dynamics of contemporary civilization (the rise of Fascism, anti-intellectualism) and the religious and philosophical foundations of Western culture (the Old Testament, the Fall, the New Testament, the Crucifixion, as well as nineteenth-century rationalism). Indeed, the very profusion of suggestive patterns in the novel should demonstrate that here is no simple allegorical reworking of the materials of *The Coral Island*, and that irrespective of Golding's initial plans, Frank Kermode properly observes: "In writing of this kind all depends upon the author's mythopoeic power to transcend the 'programme.'"[16] And in this first novel, William Golding displays "mythopoeic power" of an impressively high order. The flaws, the didactic interjections and manipulations remain. But, all in all, one may compare Golding to a puppet master who has wrought his marionettes meticulously and beautifully and led them skillfully through a captivating and frightening drama, while only occasionally distracting the audience by the movement of his strings.

3.

The Inheritors: Original Sin Defined

In his second novel, *The Inheritors*, published in 1955, Golding continues to explore man's inner nature through isolated conflict between small groups; this time the struggle, set in man's prehistoric past, pits a family of Neanderthals against a wandering tribe of Homo sapiens (the "inheritors" who will displace the Neanderthals). Here, Golding develops further, and probes more deeply, the philosophical position that he outlined in *Lord of the Flies*; that is, man is basically evil, or at least socially and morally defective.

In his first novel Golding challenged nineteenth-century rationalist notions of the civilized and the savage as embodied in Ballantyne's *Coral Island*. In *The Inheritors* he challenges another essentially nineteenth-century writer, H. G. Wells, on similar grounds, specifically indicating his intention with an epigraph from Wells's *The Outline of History*:

> . . . we know very little of the appearance of the Neanderthal man, but this . . . seems to suggest an extreme hairiness, an ugliness, or a repulsive strangeness in his appearance over and above his low forehead, his beetle brows, his ape neck, and his inferior stature. . . . Says Sir Harry Johnston, in a survey of the rise of modern man in his *Views and Reviews*: "The dim racial remembrance of such gorilla-like monsters, with cunning brains, shambling gait, hairy bodies, strong teeth, and possibly cannibalistic tendencies, may be the germ of the ogre in folklore. . . ."[1]

Oldsey and Weintraub devote considerable space to showing how Golding has used Wells's *Outline*, and a later story called "The Grisly Folk," as literary foils for *The Inheritors*, much as the Ballantyne book had served *Lord of the Flies*.[2] And here, one may hark back to Golding's remark on *Lord of the Flies* regarding "kindly savages" and the "intellectual complications" of the

21

civilized. Although the first novel provides for no such simple savages, *The Inheritors* shows just such a clash between a rudimentary and a relatively complex culture, once again exposing human depravity in such a way as to support those who may see Golding's novels as affirmations of Original Sin. My concern in this chapter will be to show how Golding uses *The Inheritors* to redefine that concept in his own terms.

The programme of *The Inheritors* again reminds one of Golding's apparent synthesis of the scientist's technique of isolated experiment, the fabulist's device of simple allegory, and the mythmaker's appeal to basic human drives and fears. And when one considers the simpleminded reactive premises of the novel— since the writings of Wells seem scarcely less straw men than those of Ballantyne—the inherent difficulties of Golding's early methods are once more evident.[3] But as in *Lord of the Flies*, Golding transcends his programme—as an artist must who uses derivative materials—by going beyond his original concept to create a work that lives in and for itself.[4] Far from merely presenting humanity for unfavorable contrast with a gentler race, Golding offers a complex, and indeed sympathetic, exploration of man's essential dilemma.

From the beginning, though, *The Inheritors* does seem a rather simplistic indictment of humanity. The book opens as the Neanderthals (or, as they call themselves, the "people") are migrating to their spring home in the mountains after a particularly hard winter spent in a cave near the sea. The bitterness of the winter and other references to climatic changes indicate the dawning of an ice age that together with other natural catastrophes, threatens the "people's" existence. Their numbers have already dwindled to a critical point: only eight remain. One cannot help noting that the group is thereby small enough to be fictionally manageable, and seems a rather carefully constructed representative sample: Mal, the old man, leader of the family, who "has the most pictures"; the old woman, never named, as befits her mysterious status as fire-bearer and priestess (the people worship Oa, a primitive fertility goddess); Ha, a young adult male who also "has many pictures"; Nil, an unintelligent female, mother of a tiny male infant (the "new one"); Fa, an apparently barren, intelligent female of independent mien; Liku, a preadolescent female; and Lok, the dull-witted protagonist.

Just as he controls their numbers, so does Golding carefully fashion the Neanderthals' nature. The people are essentially gentle creatures who exhibit the survival mechanisms of many herbivorous animals (the crude religion they practice forbids meat-eating and killing—they will eat meat only when threatened with starvation and will then eat only grubs or carrion): they are easily frightened, preferring to flee rather than fight when danger threatens. The main guide to the individual's role among the Neanderthals is expressed by the old woman's maxim: "'A woman for Oa [religious functions] and a man for the pictures in his head [rudimentary reasoning ability]'" (p. 70). James Gindin further describes Golding's people:

> For all their perceptual and intellectual limitations, the "people" have a code of ethics . . . a deep and humble sense of their own limitations, and a faith in the divine power and goodness of the earth. In addition, the "people" enjoy a family life free from fighting, guilt, and emotional squabbling. Each has his function, carefully defined and limited, each his respect for the other members of the family.[5]

The Neanderthals described above bear little resemblance to those pictured by Wells and Sir Harry Johnston; they certainly invite favorable comparison with the new people, the "inheritors," hints of whose alien presence are evident from the book's opening pages. But the people's discovery of the "inheritors" is gradual, almost annoyingly so, and allows Golding ample time to give his readers full knowledge of the people and their ways. And the fullness of that knowledge is increased by Golding's narrative approach. Leaving little doubt as to the intended focal point of the novel, and of the reader's sympathies, Golding moves beyond the relatively straightforward third-person narrative of *Lord of the Flies* to a technique that aims at emulating the viewpoint of the Neanderthals, specifically that of Lok.

Golding's creation of a prose that suggests the workings of a primitive mind is central both to interpretations of *The Inheritors* and to judgments of the novel's success or failure. But the style is, above all, characteristic of Golding's conception of his craft. He has said:

> It seems to me that there's really very little point in writing a novel unless you do something that either you suspected you couldn't do, or which you are pretty certain nobody else has tried before. I don't think there's any point in writing two books that are like each

other. . . . I see, or I bring myself to see, a certain set of circumstances in a particular way. If it is the way everybody else sees them, then there is no point in writing a book.[6]

Besides indicating the intensity of Golding's artistic commitment to originality and technical development, these remarks have been regarded by at least one critic—John Bowen—as evidence of a sort of arrogance.[7] This charge deserves consideration, and I shall return to it. At this point, suffice it to say that many of Golding's comments on his works resemble in their almost barren simplicity the bald outlines of the works themselves, which is simply to suggest that with Golding, as with other writers, one must ultimately turn to those works rather than to external commentary.

And just as *Lord of the Flies* is much more than a mere refutation of Ballantyne because of Golding's primary commitment to the convincing realization—in striking, vigorous prose—of his own fictional world, so is *The Inheritors* much more than an upending of Wellsian history, largely because of his creation of, and response to, the challenge of another highly individual narrative style. As Kinkead-Weekes and Gregor observe: "By committing himself so radically to the viewpoint of his People, by doing his utmost to ensure that he is kept out of his normal consciousness, Golding does contrive to see things new, not merely see new things."[8] And one might add that in doing so, Golding compels the reader to make a similar imaginative commitment.

Lord of the Flies, as Golding has pointed out, is a novel of self-discovery; so, too, is *The Inheritors*. Lok, the Neanderthal protagonist, learns as much about his own nature through his contacts with Homo sapiens as he does about the inheritors themselves. But the point of view adds a dimension, allowing—indeed forcing—the reader to take active part in the process of discovery, as for example when one of the "new people" shoots an arrow at Lok (note the description of the other's relatively hairless face, with its pronounced chin and forehead):

> The bushes twitched again. Lok steadied by the tree and gazed. A head and a chest faced him, half-hidden. There were white bone things above his eyes and under the mouth so that his face was longer than a face should be. The man turned sideways in the bushes and looked at Lok along his shoulder. A stick rose upright and there was

24

a lump of bone in the middle. Lok peered at the stick and the lump of bone and the small eyes in the bone things over the face. Suddenly Lok understood that the man was holding the stick out to him but neither he nor Lok could reach across the river. He would have laughed if it were not for the echo of the screaming in his head. The stick now began to grow shorter at both ends. Then it shot out to full length again.

The dead tree by Lok's ear acquired a voice.

"Clop!"

His ears twitched and he turned to the tree. By his face there had grown a twig . . .   (p. 106)

Here, Golding's description, using the simplest language, attains the level of poetry in its ability to make one see with new eyes, to share the primitive's discovery of an unfamiliar danger. And there is even a certain ironic humor in the passage, a subtle reminder of the complacent human observation, "Just imagine how we must look to them!"

Despite the fact that Golding carefully constructs his characters and situations, *The Inheritors* shows greater freedom from the overt manipulations and didacticism that marred *Lord of the Flies*. Again, this is in great part a result of the book's point of view. Just as Huck's first-person narrative in *Huckleberry Finn* largely eliminated Twain's tendency toward didactic digression, helping to make the novel Twain's most successful, so does Lok's limited viewpoint curb Golding's similar tendency. Of course, the limitation incurs certain disadvantages, among which is the ever-present danger—especially in dialogue—that translating thought and experience into rudimentary language will cause one to plunge into the "Me Tarzan, you Jane" abyss. Fortunately, Golding seldom comes even close to the brink, and more often reaches the level of poetic brilliance.

Another more important difficulty of the limited viewpoint is that Golding must necessarily draw upon resources of language unavailable to Lok's restricted faculties and experience while yet preserving the suggestion of a largely nonverbal, nonabstract mentality. The dilemma is exemplified by the following passage, in which Lok longs for Mal's wisdom: "He wished he could ask Mal what it was that joined a picture to a picture so that the last of many came out the first" (p. 96). Like Piggy's observations on natural law and supernatural phenomena, Lok's description of his own inability to think logically sounds a bit too logical and articulate. Golding's situation here reminds one of Faulkner's in *As I Lay Dying*, another novel that explores the nonverbal, intuitive depths of the human mind. Faulkner expresses the mental impressions and reactions of a character like the simpleminded Dewey Dell: "I feel the darkness rushing past my breast, past the cow; I begin to rush upon the darkness but the cow stops me and the darkness rushes on upon the sweet blast of her moaning breath, filled with wood and with silence."[9] Ultimately, one must concede writers such license, since refusal to do so would effectively cut off their means of dealing with areas of experience that constitute the very medium of human life.

As the boys' descent into savagery in *Lord of the Flies* is steady, gathering momentum with each passing day, so in *The Inheritors* the people's downfall is progressively hastened by each hint of or confrontation with the new people. The first indication of the inheritors' presence is the disappearance of a log bridge that the people have used for many years on their journey to their spring home. Although the realization evades the people, their log has been taken by the inheritors, who have floated it downriver to their island camp on the edge of the waterfall as fuel for a bonfire.

Faced with finding a new way across the water or leading the people on a long detour around a swamp, Mal probes back into his memory for a "picture" of how the first crossingplace had been created. He directs the family in placing a recently fallen tree where the old bridge had lain, which requires Ha to enter the water, an experience particularly abhorrent to the people. During the crossing Mal falls into the water, bringing on a chill that leads eventually to his death. The crossing accomplished, the people proceed to their spring quarters, a cave in a cliff overlooking the waterfall and the island where the inheritors are camped.

The episode of the log bridge, simple as it is, introduces several vital thematic and symbolic elements into the novel. The missing log is the first of many old and trusted features of the people's life that begin to fail them or to disappear because of the new people. And the water becomes a symbol of the many new and repellent things that the people will learn or be required to do (Ha's immersion), and of the dangers of thinking like a man, the dangers of knowledge (Mal's fall, and his subsequent death). In almost every crucial episode of the novel to follow, a tree or the river or both are central features. The religious contexts from which Golding draws these symbols are readily apparent, and further indicate his determination to give his novels the deep human appeal of myth. The log represents the Tree of Knowledge which, of course, leads to sin, or more importantly, to a sinful—or human—nature. The river leads to the waterfall, for which one may read the Fall, of man or Neanderthal.

Lok, describing the new people, whose camp Golding fortuitously locates on the island below the waterfall, says, "They are like the river and the fall; nothing stands against them" (p. 195). And the humans are indeed "people of the Fall." Their Original Sin, as Golding pictures it, is embodied in the evolutionary step that has made them thinking creatures, in the elaborate survival mechanism that is the human brain. But here is no simple contrast between the innocent and the fallen, for the issue of guilt is surely complicated by Golding's evolutionary interpretation of the Fall. The inheritors are as much victims of their own nature as are the Neanderthals they slaughter. Golding's emphasis on this point is slight through all but the novel's final chapter, but the theme is implicit from the beginning.

Why then does Golding emphasize the Neanderthals' point of view, if not for the primary purpose of attacking rationalist notions of man's sinless nature? The answer to this question again requires the preliminary observation that Golding often seems to "transcend his programme." The epigraph from Wells indicates a large measure of ironic intent on Golding's part, but a thorough examination of the Neanderthal viewpoint shows that his purposes are far wider. The opportunity to see through Lok's "innocent" eyes brings home more sharply to the reader man's propensity for evil and destruction, but it should also bring several other realizations.

The first such realization is that—innocent and appealing as they are—the Neanderthals are ill-equipped for survival. In fact, they are already on the way toward extinction before the advent of the inheritors. Allusions early in the novel indicate that the people are a dying race, prey to the changes in climate and physical environment that herald the coming ice age, as well as to more specific catastrophes. More importantly, though, the people have been generally unable to heed these signs because of their limited powers of abstraction. As Fa says early in the novel, "'To-day is like yesterday and to-morrow'" (p. 46). And a few pages later, after food has been found, the people's reaction is noteworthy: "The people were silent. Life was fulfilled, there was no need to look farther for food, to-morrow was secure and the day after that so remote that no one would bother to think of it" (p. 61).

Then, too, Golding more than once hints that creative or abstract thought challenges the people's basic and distrustful conservatism, suggesting thereby that their mental range is limited more by choice than by lack of potential. This point is illustrated by the old woman's reaction to Fa's halting attempt to formulate a means of carrying water from place to place in sea shells:

> The old woman was leaning towards Fa. Then she swayed back, lifted both hands off the earth and poised on her skinny hams. Slowly, deliberately, her face changed to that face she would make suddenly if Liku strayed too near the flaunting colors of the poison berry. Fa shrank before her and put her hands up to her face. The old woman spoke.
> "That is a new thing."   (p. 63)

The foregoing suggests that the Neanderthals are marked for extinction because, like most animal species, they are controlled by their environment. Their more obviously human traits are insufficiently developed to enable them to change that environment. Thus, if *The Inheritors* is an ironic revelation of man's fallen state, it also demonstrates that there seems no alternative to that state, no hope of a return to innocence. In Golding's world the meek cannot inherit the earth.

However, there is further irony: the people—the innocents— are apparently doomed to eventual extinction by their essentially animal response to their environment, but are actually led to their downfall by their human traits. Water, identified early in the novel with the inheritors and with the "sin" of knowledge, is also a source of fascination for the people, as when Liku demands that Lok swing her on a branch dangerously near the water's edge. Lok later acknowledges this vague fascination and specifically relates it to the inheritors: "The other people with their many pictures were like water that at once horrifies and at the same time dares and invites a man to go near it" (p. 126).

Perhaps the most striking indication of water's importance in the novel's scheme, and of Golding's ability to enrich and deepen his symbolic visions beyond his original conceptions, may be seen in the concluding section of chapter five. Ha, the first of the people to make contact with the inheritors, has been killed; Mal is dead; Nil and the Old Woman have been killed, and Liku and the "new one" kidnapped in a raid by the inheritors on the people's camp. Lok, hearing Liku's screams coming from the island, crawls far out over the stream on a mass of overhanging branches in an attempt to reach her, and while hanging upside down on this precarious perch, he experiences a nightmarish vision:

> Then, because he no longer moved, the branches began to bend under him. They swayed outwards and down so that his head was lower than his feet. He sank, gibbering, and the water rose, bringing a Lok-face with it. There was a tremble of light over the Lok-face but he could see the teeth. Below the teeth, a weed-tail was moving backwards and forwards, more than the length of a man each time. But everything else under the teeth and the ripple was remote and dark. . . .
> The weed tail was shortening. The green tip was withdrawing up river. There was a darkness that was consuming the other end. The darkness became a thing of complex shape, of sluggish and dreamlike movement. Like the specks of dirt, it turned over but not aimlessly. It was touching near the root of the weed-tail, bending the tail, turning over, rolling up the tail towards him. The arms moved a little and the eyes shone as dully as the stones. They revolved with the body, gazing at the surface, at the width of deep water and the hidden bottom with no trace of life or speculation. A skein of weed drew across the face and the eyes did not blink. The body turned with the same smooth and heavy motion as the river itself until its back was towards him rising along the weed-tail. The head turned towards him with dreamlike slowness, rose in the water, came towards his face. . . .
> . . . She was ignoring the injuries to her body, her mouth was open, the tongue showing and the specks of dirt were circling slowly in and out as though it had been nothing but a hole in a stone. Her eyes swept across the bushes, across his face, looked through him without seeing him, rolled away and were gone.   (pp. 107–9)

This section perfectly demonstrates Golding's ability to describe the physical world from a startlingly oblique angle that, combined with masterly presentation of detail and tight rhythmic

control, gives his highly organized symbolic concepts both substance and arresting ambiguity. Here, Lok comes face to face not
merely with death in the shape of an old woman—a matriarch
representing a simpler way of life—but also with himself. His
reflected face hovers above depths that are "remote and dark,"
the depths of his own mind as well as of the river—depths that
the death of his mother will force him to plumb. Here is Lok's
first insight into the complexity that exists not only without, but
also within. The simple life is over.

Despite Lok's vision, the initiative for further action passes to
Fa, who explains to him: "'Lok has no pictures in his head. . . .
Do what I say. Do not say: "Fa do this." I will say: "Lok do
this." I have many pictures'" (p. 117). And like Adam, Lok allows himself to be persuaded. Continuing the ironic Adam and
Eve parallel, one sees that the only serpent in this Eden is man.
And like the serpent, man attracts this primitive couple, although their desire to rescue Liku and the "new one" is a powerful motivating force in the action that follows.

To this end Fa conceives the notion of lodging a tree at the lip
of the fall as a bridge to the island. This done, the two people
cross the bridge and, under cover of night, descend the cliff to
the inheritors' camp. They find the new people in the midst of a
primitive animal-worshiping rite, and the fear and anger that
greet the two "forest devils" (as the humans call the Neanderthals) remind one sharply of the boys' reaction to Simon in *Lord
of the Flies*, when he interrupts a similar rite and is likewise
mistaken for the Beast. Unlike Simon, Lok and Fa escape death
for the time being; but this scene has, nonetheless, similar implications.

Meanwhile, having recrossed the river, Lok and Fa enact another of Golding's ironic reversals of myth, as Lok (Adam) convinces Fa (Eve) that they should climb a huge dead tree from
which, unseen, they can watch the new people, much as Golding, himself, had watched the adult world in his childhood
from a large chestnut tree. Fa, who sees clearly the threat of the
new people, wishes to leave Liku and the "new one" captive and
retreat to the old life, to the cave by the sea. Lok's motivations
in this reversal of the Tree of Knowledge myth are, however,
unassailable. Since Fa is apparently barren (see pp. 70, 105, 133,

207), her wish to retreat is unrealistic, a sure path to extinction. Therefore, Lok's wish to attempt a rescue is both logical and admirable.

In any case, when the new people move their camp across the river to the forest's edge, the two Neanderthals are treated to a view of Homo sapiens that amounts to a catalog of the seven deadly sins. Again using the primitive viewpoint to full advantage, Golding portrays man in all of his various states of wickedness, weakness, and vanity. And during this extended revelation of human folly, Golding produces his most ironic commentary on the epigraph from Wells's *Outline*. The humans, facing starvation, threaten to kill and eat their priest-leader, Marlan, whom they blame for their evil luck. The old man, however, convinces them that the "forest devils" are to blame, and that the tribe might best serve both religious and physical needs by killing and eating Liku. Thus, Wells is refuted, and the ogre located within man, himself.

This neat reversal, seeming again to point to overly simplistic tendencies in Golding's approach, demands closer examination. Cannibalism, monstrous as it may seem, seems necessary to the new people's survival. And Liku, alien and grotesque, is the logical victim. Furthermore, the religious aspect of the deed—especially in the light of modern anthropological and psychological studies of ritual killing—becomes extremely significant. Ritual killing and sacrifice are fundamental elements of man's actual and mythological past. Most often they involve either or both of these considerations: the rationalization of an essentially monstrous deed by investing it with religious significance; and the use of a sacrificial proxy (or scapegoat) to represent the group, or its misdeeds.[10]

In Christianity, the deed (the Crucifixion) is the more monstrous because Christ fills at once the role of scapegoat and bearer of Divine Truth. And again one is reminded of Simon who likewise takes on both roles, and whose truth is the identification of the Beast as "only us." In *The Inheritors*, Golding repeats the pattern with deeper implications. Lok and Fa temporarily escape the fate of Simon when they blunder into the inheritors' ceremony. Liku, however, does not. Golding's purpose becomes clearer in the following excerpt from the novel's

Of Earth and Darkness

final chapter, in which the child Tanakil, driven mad by the cannibalistic killing of Liku and by fear of the "forest devils," speaks from her madness:

> "Liku!"
> Tuami heard Marlan whisper to him from by the mast.
> "That is the devil's name. Only she may speak it."   (p. 228)

The slaughtered innocent is once more equated with evil, and the primal murder is at once legitimized and repressed. Again, the real source of evil is man himself, and the scapegoat—like Christ and Simon—is the bearer of that truth, for her name—certainly no accident—is Liku (like/you). In Golding's view, the Fall is both fortunate and unfortunate, and the ritual killing a source of both redemption and damnation.

As the inheritors mistake innocent for devil, Lok (like so many victimized primitives) mistakes the "new man" for god. After an abortive attempt to rescue Liku (who he believes is still alive) and the "new one," Lok finds himself separated from Fa, who has been wounded. Alone, he discovers in himself the budding powers of abstraction, of "likeness." And those powers, that have as often seduced man into errors of logic as into flights of genius, lead him to the following conclusion concerning the new people: "'They are like Oa'" (p. 195). This mistaken notion that has led so many primitives into degrading emulation of civilized man leads Lok and Fa down the same path. Reunited, they return to the new people's now-abandoned camp, where they sample, with ludicrous results, a crude alcoholic honey-beverage that has been left them as a sacrifice by the fleeing humans. At the climax of this scene, Golding again underscores the fact that the people have fallen, as Lok announces in his drunkenness: "'I am one of the new people'" (p. 204).

However, Lok and Fa have little opportunity to test their emerging humanness. In another unsuccessful rescue attempt, Fa is wounded, then carried over the waterfall to her death as she sits, dazed, in a floating tangle of branches. Lok, left alone, an Adam whose Eve has been taken from him, succumbs to his own sense of irretrievable loss, literally curling up to die in the shadow of the people's mountain cave, beneath a grotesque totemic picture of himself left by the humans as a token of appeasement to the "forest devils." Thus, when Lok dies beneath an avalanche caused by the spring thaw, the Neanderthals become extinct while still in a state of relative innocence. But this fact, and Golding's generally sympathetic treatment of the Neanderthals, should not blind the reader to the knowledge that the people, had they been spared, must surely have followed the "human" path. Indeed, in the transitional section that ends chapter eleven, Lok becomes—in a shift of viewpoint—merely "the red creature." Having surrendered in the struggle to survive, he becomes a figure less tragic than pathetic.

This transitional episode is highly effective, preparing the reader for the further shift to the human viewpoint that occurs in the novel's concluding chapter. Without compromising the reader's sympathy for the Neanderthals, Golding nonetheless manages, by making Lok's death pathetic, to focus attention on the human situation, which attains tragic significance. Just as Lok gained a measure of self-awareness, so does Tuami, the tribal artist of the new people. Again, Golding uses the artist-figure as perceiver of truth. And again, the visionary seems largely powerless in the dynamic world of human action. When the chapter begins, Tuami is busy sharpening a knife to be used as a weapon against Marlan, the priest-leader of the tribe and Tuami's rival for the voluptuous Vivani; but Tuami is daunted by the thought of murder. Guilt has entered man's world.[11] Like Lok, upside down over deep water, Tuami is vaguely conscious of the change: "I am like a pool, he thought, some tide has filled me, the sand is swirling, the waters are obscured and strange things are creeping out of the cracks and crannies of my mind" (p. 227). Tuami, however, is more perceptive than Lok, and manages to grasp the truth of his—of man's—plight. Looking at the knife he is making, he thinks: "What was the use of sharpening it against a man? Who would sharpen a point against the darkness of the world?" (p. 231).

This somber realization, reminiscent of Ralph's lament at the end of *Lord of the Flies*, is not Golding's final word. He carries his programme a step further, suggesting that if man is a guilty and destructive creature, he also possesses the potential for creativity and, perhaps, redemption. Marlan, still mistakenly externalizing man's dilemma, attempts to reassure himself and the others concerning the "devils": "'They keep to the mountains or the darkness under the trees. We will keep to the water and the plains. We shall be safe from the tree-darkness'" (p. 231). But Tuami, watching the "new one" and Vivani, comes closer to the truth:

> Then the devil appeared, arse upward, his little rump pushing against the nape of [Vivani's] neck. . . . Tuami let the ivory drop from his hands. The sun shone on the head and the rump and quite suddenly everything was all right again and the sands had sunk back to the bottom of the pool. The rump and the head fitted each other and made a shape you could feel with your hands. They were waiting in the rough ivory of the knife-haft that was so much more important than the blade. They were an answer, the frightened, angry love of the woman and the ridiculous, intimidating rump that was wagging at her head, they were a password.   (p. 233)

The possibility of redemption exists in commitment to creation rather than destruction; for Golding the primary symbol of creation is the artist, who can also interpret for us, if he is heeded, the truths of the human condition. But the knife has a blade, as well as a haft. And Golding knows that the innocent and the devil are one, that man has charted a course over waters that are wide and deep. Thus, the novel concludes with a sobering reminder for Tuami: "He peered forward past the sail to see what lay at the other end of the lake, but it was so long, and there was such a flashing from the water that he could not see if the line of darkness had an ending" (p. 233).

Tuami's insight, however tentative, is more complex and far-reaching than that given to Ralph at the end of *Lord of the Flies*. Whereas Ralph is weeping, left with a sense of the "darkness of man's heart," Tuami realizes that man is compounded of both light and darkness and is able to sense, however dimly, "an answer, . . . a password." There is irony here as well, since Tuami and his insight are lost in prehistory, and Ralph's childish confusion and sorrow are set in a time yet to come. Nevertheless, the answer is there for those who have eyes to see it. Clearly, in his second novel, Golding deepens and extends the themes that he developed in *Lord of the Flies*. In addition to creating what amounts to a tour de force of description and point of view, he shows in *The Inheritors* a surer grasp of his symbolic structure, weaving together myth, religion, anthropology, psychology, and sociology to produce a definition of Original Sin far more complex than the simple moral formulas he is often accused of embodying in his fiction. Further, he accomplishes his difficult thematic task in the context of a thoroughly engrossing story and manages to curtail in large measure the tendency to didacticism that mars *Lord of the Flies*.

Many critics persist, however, in seeing Golding's work in simplistic terms, sometimes even berating him for those elements in his fiction that point most clearly to its depth and range. James Gindin, for example, seized on Golding's unfortunate use of the word *gimmick* in connection with the endings of several of his novels, and had this to say on the final chapter of *The Inheritors*:

> The "gimmick," the switch in point of view, merely repeats what the rest of the novel has already demonstrated. Awareness and rational intelligence are still inextricably connected with human sin, and the "gimmick" at the end of the novel breaks the unity without adding relevant perspective.[12]

This 1960 reading of the novel, obviously seeing a mere refutation of Wells, and missing the guarded optimism introduced in the final chapter, exemplifies the superficial reaction of many early Golding critics, even those who viewed his novels favorably. And perhaps such superficial criticism is more than a little responsible for Golding's early preoccupation with the theme of survival, to which he returns again in his third novel, *Pincher Martin*, while at the same time moving closer to conventional fiction and narrowing his focus from groups to an individual. Nonetheless, *The Inheritors* stands by itself as a major achievement, testifying emphatically to the originality and power of the author's vision.

4.

Pincher Martin:
Concession, Restatement, Assertion

In *Pincher Martin*, which appeared in 1956, Golding once more takes up the survival motif that had dominated his first two novels. In writing this tale of a shipwrecked sailor's struggle against death, Golding was perhaps motivated by a desire to clarify his philosophical position, a position that his early critics mistakenly found either patently obvious or willfully obscure and evasive. However, those critics had also suggested that Golding's fictional approach smacked of eccentricity, and despite its obvious seriousness and artistry had often looked askance at what seemed its elements of science fiction.[1] *Pincher Martin* appears to be a transitional work in which Golding attempts once again to explain his views, while at the same time creating a novel more acceptable to critics of his unorthodox methods without compromising his own artistic integrity. The difficulty of such a task is fairly obvious, and it is therefore unsurprising that *Pincher Martin* initially drew more critical fire than did *Lord of the Flies* or *The Inheritors*; however, an examination of the novel's transitional status provides considerable insight into both the entire Golding canon and his approach to his art.

The bare outline of *Pincher Martin* is simple: Christopher Hadley Martin, an officer in the Royal Navy during World War II, is shipwrecked on a tiny island in mid-Atlantic when his ship is torpedoed; the bulk of the novel deals with his ultimately doomed struggle to survive until rescue comes.[2] Although Golding retains the survival theme, *Pincher Martin* differs from its predecessors in a number of significant ways, not the least of which is its individual focus. Both *Lord of the Flies* and *The Inheritors*, while concerned with individual characters, are plotted largely in terms of group dynamics and interactions, with basic actions and thematic concerns developing from the juxtaposition of opposing groups. Thus, Golding's third novel emerges as an amalgam common to his previous novels and elements that seem to answer in some respects those critics who viewed his fictional world as too far removed from contemporary reality. Here are the isolation, the harsh struggle for existence, the brilliant description, and the moral intensity of the earlier books; yet here, too, in the form of flashbacks to Martin's past, are contemporary society and a "typical" protagonist.

The initially harsh critical response to *Pincher Martin* was based, however, on another characteristic Golding touch: the novel's final few pages make clear—in a startling turnabout—that Martin's ordeal has in fact occurred after his death, demanding that it be treated as a metaphysical, rather than a physical, experience. Numerous reviewers assailed the novel's ending as another Golding *gimmick*, recalling Ambrose Bierce's "An Occurrence at Owl Creek Bridge."[3] And although later critics have more acutely perceived the unifying role of the ending and rightly assessed *Pincher Martin* as a brilliantly conceived and executed work, the fact of those early reactions adds an instructive dimension to a consideration of the novel's transitional status. Before discussing the significance of the ending, however, I should like to examine in some detail the ways in which Golding uses Christopher Martin's ordeal as a vehicle of restatement and concession, with a view to illuminating the final assertion of his own artistic approach that the controversial conclusion represents.

The Inheritors takes up Golding's thematic concerns where *Lord of the Flies* leaves off, redefining and clarifying. And *Pincher Martin*, with its programme of individual isolation, proceeds from the conclusion of *The Inheritors*. This suggests that the evolutionary step that made man a thinking, creative creature also produced the isolation of the individual human mind, concomitant elevation of the individual will, and the solitary burden of loneliness and guilt that serves as bitter leavening to Tuami's brief access of optimistic faith in creativity. As Tuami realizes, his knife has a killing blade as well as a potentially beautiful haft, and the difference in focus separating the beautiful from the deadly is slight. Viewed in broad terms, Christopher

Martin and his saintly friend, Nathaniel Walterson, represent the extremes of this duality.

With the development of civilization, itself evolved to ensure human survival, comes a notion that Freud and Marx (complementing each other and Darwin) have made a modern commonplace: namely, that the patterns of nature will be repeated in civilization through sublimation or socioeconomic pressure or both; that the survival instinct will make itself apparent in social terms. *Lord of the Flies* and *The Inheritors* suggest this view of civilization; in *Pincher Martin* it is pivotal. Man neither can nor should attempt to escape his urge for, and chief means of, survival; but as Golding's first two novels suggest, when creativity turns itself to rationalization it becomes delusive and—in moral terms—highly dangerous. To use an example that Golding himself might well cite, the sublimated instinct is capable of convincing itself that the slaughter of six million Jews is somehow necessary to survival. *Pincher Martin* is, from its individual focal point, an acting out of this view in both social and metaphysical terms.

Golding's concern with the dangers of rationalism appears at full force in *Pincher Martin*. The novel begins abruptly, with the chaotic perceptions of a drowning man: "He was struggling in every direction, he was the centre of the writhing and kicking knot of his own body. There was no up or down, no light and no air. He felt his mouth open of itself and the shrieked word burst out. 'Help!'"[4] But there is no help. The reader is plunged at once, with little time for reflection, into Martin's desperate fight against death. The first calming note in this frantic scene is, importantly, Martin's formation of a lucid mental image, an analogy for survival (pp. 8–9). As Jack I. Biles and Carl R. Kropf point out in an essay on *Pincher Martin*, this image of the Cartesian diver in a jam jar, which reminds Martin of his life belt, is at the heart of the novel's theme.[5] Like Descartes, the epitome of rationalism, Martin takes for his guiding principle the phrase, "Cogito, ergo sum," and he attempts to create for himself "a little world . . . quite separate but which one could control" (p. 8). The battle lines are thus drawn between Martin and the universe. As he later declares to the "quiet sea": "'I don't claim to be a hero. But I've got health and education and intelligence. I'll beat you'" (p. 77). From the very first, then,

Martin's situation is archetypal, and when he chooses as the stage for his drama a barren rock, the Promethean image suggests the metaphysical dimensions that develop later in the novel.

The words *stage* and *drama* are particularly appropriate to Martin's attempt to avoid dying. First, they are apt because, as one learns in the book's final chapter, Martin's rock is a construction of his own mind, the "centre" of his being, "that was so nakedly the center of everything that it could not even examine itself" (p. 45). The centre creates the rock out of "the memory of an aching tooth" and tries to surround Martin with a world that will shut out the reality of his death, using the raw materials of his recollection; the theater in which the play is staged is the "globe" of Martin's skull (one may assume that the word, which Golding uses in several places, is indeed a pun). E. C. Bufkin, in an essay entitled "*Pincher Martin*: William Golding's Morality Play," shows how theatrical terms pervade the novel, and how Martin, whose peacetime profession was acting, continually casts himself in self-consciously dramatic situations and roles.[6]

Indeed, one of the flashbacks to Martin's past is a scene in which he is asked to play a double role in a morality play; already cast as a shepherd, he is forced to accept a part as one of the Seven Deadly Sins. Martin objects to this and Pete, the play's producer, whom Martin is openly cuckolding, replies, "'Double, old man? Everybody's doubling. . . .'" (p. 118). Martin then reluctantly accompanies Pete to the costumiere's workroom, referred to as "the crypt," to choose his second role. As they walk downstairs, Pete remarks to the play's director: "'Curious feeling to the feet this carpet over stone, George. Something thick and costly, just allowing your senses to feel the basic stuff beneath.'" Immediately after he gestures at the costumes: "'There they are, Chris, all in a row. What about it?'" (p. 119). Although Chris tries to pick a part irrelevant to his true character, Pete makes him take the role of Greed. "'Darling, it's simply *you*,'" says Pete, and "introduces" Martin to the Greed mask with pointed reference to the actor himself:

> "This painted bastard here takes anything he can lay his hands on. Not food, Chris, that's far too simple. He takes the best part, the best seat, the most money, the best notice, the best woman. He was born

with his mouth and his flies open and both hands out to grab. He's a
cosmic case of the bugger who gets his penny and someone else's
bun."   (p. 120)

The point is obvious: in the costumiere's "crypt" Martin's producer strips him to the "basic stuff beneath," just as God will do
at the moment of death.

The above-described scene is centrally significant to the novel
in other ways, too. Here Golding introduces the motif of Martin's fear of cellars, which has persisted since childhood and returns continually to plague his creation of a script for survival.
Prompted by the fact that the cellar of his boyhood home (like
Golding's) was next to a graveyard, this fear is rooted in Martin's refusal to accept his mortality, an even more basic and undeniable part of his nature than his greed, which is a response to
the fear of death.[7] I shall discuss presently Golding's continuing
identification of Pete, the producer, with God and with immi-
nent death; suffice it to say that Golding uses scenes involving
Pete, as he does most features of Martin's past, as symbolic ana-
logues to Martin's "present" on the rock.

Another important aspect of the mask scene returns one to a
consideration of Martin's profession. Although, as Pete points
out, "'Everybody's doubling'" (that is, every man plays two
roles, one being his basic nature), one notes that Martin's other
role—besides Greed—is that of a shepherd, obviously not a
principal character in the morality play. This fact, and Golding's
explicit identification of Martin with the sin of greed, seems
worthy of closer examination. E. C. Bufkin points out, with reference to Gerald Vann's *The Heart of Man*, that "Martin's particular vice—greed—stems, as does all sin, from the original sin
of pride, *superbia*."[8] And Martin's solitary defiance of death, of
God's will, certainly argues pride. But pictured in flashbacks as
a man whose pride—or hubris—is made manifest in small-
minded grasping, Martin is far removed from the pose of tragic
hero that he attempts on his rocky stage. Golding has said of
Martin as a fallen man: "He's fallen more than most. In fact I
went out of my way to damn Pincher as much as I could by
making him the nastiest type I could think of, and I was very
interested to see how critics all over the place said, 'Well yes, we
are like that.'"[9] Whereas the Greek tragedians, with whom Golding is well-acquainted, clearly intend their heroes to represent

man in the larger sense, Golding here seems to have something quite different in mind. Martin is no more Everyman in Golding's morality play than in Pete's; but like the "Pincher" he is, Martin attempts to usurp the role.

The most that is said for Martin as an actor, with his smooth looks, his "wavy hair and profile" (p. 119), is that he is his company's "best bloody juvenile" (p. 135), hardly an image adequate to tragic heroism. Indeed, in a passage already quoted, Martin says, "'I don't claim to be a hero.'" An actor like Chris hears and sees the tragic hero only as a bystander, whether in the wings or onstage; thus, his concept of the role is disjointed and fragmentary. And it is as an actor, already at one remove from the creative process, that Martin tries to usurp not only the role of tragic hero, but also of playwright, of the creator himself. Such a dual role would be too much for the best of men. For Martin, it results in parody—he is both parodic hero and parodic creator.

And here a similarity is suggested between Martin and Jack Merridew of *Lord of the Flies*. Jack, another parodic Prometheus, steals fire (in the form of a pair of spectacles) from Piggy, a parodic Zeus, just as the equally opportunistic Martin steals Pete's wife. Piggy and Pete, however, correspond to modern notions of God, weakened by rationalism and susceptible to opportunistic victimization; the true God, the One who comprehends the world's darkness, bides His time until the final reckoning.

In any case, Martin's efforts to sustain the dual role of hero and creator are underlined—and diminished—by numerous parallels to religion, myth, and literature. Kinkead-Weekes and Gregor, as well as James Baker, show at length that Martin's sojourn on the rock ironically parallels the seven days of creation in Genesis, during which Martin desperately tries to stave off the nothingness of death by manufacturing his own world, first creating light and air, then the rock, and so forth, to the moment at which he "creates" God in his own image.[10] First, however, submerging the dangerous admission of open competition with God, Martin sees himself as a latter-day Crusoe, surveying his "estate" (pp. 77–78), listing methodically the "facts" of his condition and the requisites for survival (pp. 81–82), and busying himself with "'netting down this rock with names and taming it'" (p. 86).[11] But the world of Defoe and Crusoe is too prosaic and substantial to remain related for long to Martin's improvised and illusionary island. He is forced to switch to simpler roles, roles less dependent on the order of the natural world, but roles that by their very archetypal nature bring him inexorably closer to an admission of his actual situation.

Greek myth enters Martin's increasingly frenzied drama, first suggesting itself to the reader in the Promethean image of solitary man on barren rock. Martin, to whom his own identity is precious above all, invokes the classical names and roles only when his self-created world begins to crumble, bracing himself for the last ditch effort to survive which begins with a self-administered enema:

> "I am Atlas. I am Prometheus."
> He felt himself loom, gigantic on the rock. His jaws clenched, his chin sank. He became a hero for whom the impossible was an achievement.   (p. 164)

The enema itself becomes a piece of theater, accompanied by background music—"snatches of Tchaikovsky, Wagner, Holst" (p. 164). Such theatricality serves at once to underline how far the imagined scene is removed from both physical reality and the heroic dimensions of myth, however much Martin may be said to possess the hubris of the classical hero.

As his illusion suffers further breakdowns, Martin changes roles more often, frantically switching back and forth between the Shakespearean and the classical. When he decides on madness as an explanation of his inadequacy as a creator, he thinks: "There was still a part that could be played—there was the Bedlamite, Poor Tom. . . ." (pp. 177–78). Martin's decision to adopt the role of the disguised Edgar, from *King Lear*, is doubly ironic: first, Edgar *feigns* madness (as does Martin) to escape the *unjust* wrath of his father (and Martin feels likewise put upon); second, if Martin resembles any character from *King Lear*, it is the bastard Edmund who, like Martin, bears allegiance to a philosophy of egotism and unchecked natural impulse: "Thou, Nature, art my goddess; to thy law / My services are bound" (*King Lear*, 1.2. 1–2). Next, Martin chooses to play Lear, himself—"'Now I am thin and weak. . . . My eyes are dull stones'" (p. 188, see *King Lear*, 3.2. 18–19)—but his misquotation merely shows his unsuitability for the role, and the suggestion of weakness cannot be long tolerated by the centre.

So it is back to Prometheus: "'Hoé, hoé! Thor's lightning challenges me! Flash after flash, rippling spurts of white fire, bolts flung at Prometheus, blinding white, white, white, searing, the aim of the sky at the man on the rock—'"(pp. 188–89). And again, to the accompaniment of "storm music," he shouts, "'Ajax! Prometheus!'" (p. 192).

But his inability to hold together the increasingly incoherent illusion quickly forces him to return to the pose of insanity (p. 193). This allows him to accept as hallucinatory the dialogue with God that follows (pp. 194–97). And finally he acknowledges his attempt to usurp God's role as Creator: "'On the sixth day he created God. Therefore I permit you to use nothing but my own vocabulary. In his own image created he Him'" (p. 196). But although the visual aspect of the scene may be Martin's projection, the voice is God's, and Martin is asked to consider the reality of his death. When Martin responds with, "'I will not consider! I have created you and I can create my own heaven,'" God's reply spells final doom for Chris and his second-hand creation: "'You have created it'" (p. 196). Abruptly diminished from pretensions, however ironic, to the stature of Milton's Satan, Martin petulantly echoes Adam—"Did I request thee, Maker, from my clay, / To mould me man?" (*Paradise Lost*, 10:743–44)—by demanding, "'If I ate them [the people he has used and victimized in life], who gave me a mouth?'" (p. 197). Like Milton's God (see *Paradise Lost*, 10:763–64), Golding's refuses to respond, only saying, "'There is no answer in your vocabulary'" (p. 197).

Unlike Adam, however, Martin remains unregenerate, refuses to accept freely God's will. He returns to the posture of mad, tragic, hero, again misquoting *King Lear*:

> Rage, roar, spout!
> Let us have wind, rain, hail, gouts of blood,
> Storms and tornadoes . . .
> . . . hurricanes and typhoons . . .
>   (p. 197, see *King Lear*, 3.2. 1–6)

The profoundest irony, however, in Martin's selection of this particular speech for misquotation is that it ends as follows:

> . . . And thou, all-shaking thunder,
> Strike flat the thick rotundity o' th' world,
> Crack Nature's moulds, all germains spill
>   at once,
> That make ingrateful man!   (*King Lear*, 3.2. 6–9)

Though Martin fails to conclude the speech, God does, destroying absolutely the illusory world and reducing Martin, after his last, silent, pseudo-Promethean, pseudo-Satanic, cry—"'I shit on your heaven!'" (p. 200)—to his final primeval role, that of a pair of huge lobster claws, grimly clinging to life while God's all-destroying black lightning advances: "playing over them, prying for a weakness, wearing them away in a compassion that was timeless and without mercy" (p. 201).

The preceding discussion by no means exhausts the literary and mythical-religious parallels that may be seen in *Pincher Martin*. E. C. Bufkin points out several significant mythical-religious associations to be considered with respect to Martin's name.[12] And Oldsey and Weintraub postulate literary connections that include Eliot and Hemingway, examine the novel's previously mentioned resemblance to Bierce's "An Occurrence at Owl Creek Bridge," and discuss another possible source of Golding's inspiration in *Pincher Martin*: *O. D.*, a minor adventure narrative of World War I by "Taffrail" (H. T. Dorling).[13]

But however many parallels Golding may have had in mind in *Pincher Martin*, one thing seems clear: Martin's own conscious and half-conscious emulation of heroic roles serves to advance, through irony, Golding's elaborated restatement of his views on the use and misuse of human creativity. Martin, like so many others, has grown up in a world in which creativity is mainly applied secondhand: just as technology has become the dominant scientific mode of the modern age, pragmatism has dominated modern thought; the search for truth by the creative thinker has been replaced largely by various forms of rationalization. And Pincher Martin carries this proposition to its ultimate conclusion: rather than employing his creative powers in the search for truth, he instead devotes them to the construction of a monumental lie. The lie is ultimately doomed merely by its untruth, but also because Martin's mode of creation is secondhand, using materials he fails to understand—how could he, when he perceives things only in relation to their usefulness to himself? The modern consciousness, Golding seems to say, has sought ways of avoiding basic truths. Despite the rationalistic approach—and because of it—the modern mind has steadily refused to confront the darker side of human experience, a side that ancient myth and religion confront squarely. Survival is to be desired; but to fear death so much as to attempt denying its actuality is to begin a process of delusion that sees, as does Martin, a kind of death in every denial of individual desire.

Thus, Christopher Martin may be seen as Everyman only in a contemporary and limited sense. Like modern man, Martin is an actor who has shrunk through rationalism to a stature far removed from that of the mythical and heroic characters he attempts to play. He has shrunk because his self-concern makes him oblivious to cosmic realities such as death; and his God, steadily attacked by the forces of rationalism, has shrunk, too. Pete, Chris's producer, is typical of the rationalist God, no longer a ruling influence in life. Golding makes the ironic identification between Pete and the real God explicit in chapter twelve, where Martin, accustomed to manipulating superior forces to his own ends, confuses Pete with the powerful God he now faces, and attempts to influence this Pete-God as he had done in life, through Pete's wife, Helen (in the form of a woman-figure he has created on the rock): "'I wouldn't ask anyone but you because the rock is fixed and if he'll only let it alone it'll last forever. After all, my sweet, you're his wife'" (p. 178).

But, in this parody of the temptation of Eve, Martin's notion of roles is hopelessly confused. And the true God is not to be swayed. In fact, Martin's attempt to avoid service in the war through Helen's intercession had also failed (see pp. 154–55). And Pete, himself, weak as he is, analyzes Martin's true nature, both in the Greed-mask scene and in another, which introduces the symbolic motif of the Chinese box that pervades the novel. While drunk, Pete describes for Martin the Chinese custom of burying a tin box containing a dead fish, which breeds maggots who consume first the fish, then each other, leaving "'one huge, successful maggot. Rare dish.'" Pete then pointedly compares Chris to the maggot: "'Have you ever heard a spade knocking on the side of a tin box, Chris? Boom! Boom! Just like thunder'" (p. 136). And in the novel's intricate symbolic structure, it is the thunder of a giant spade against a tin box (associated, too, with the coffins in the cellar) that accompanies the destructive black lightning of God which threatens Martin on his rock.

45

The source of the black lightning that symbolizes death for Martin is a statement by Nathaniel Walterson, Chris's saintly friend, who succeeds in winning Mary Lovell, the girl for whom Martin feels an obsessive lust. Nathaniel, a mystic in the mold of Simon, concerns himself, as Chris does not, with the reality of death. And in one flashback Nat discusses with Martin the "technique of dying into heaven" (p. 71). "'Take us as we are now,'" says Nat, "'and heaven would be sheer negation. Without form and void. You see? A sort of black lightning destroying everything that we call life'" (p. 70). Martin retains this horrifying image, his only concept of the afterlife, during his struggle on the rock.

Nathaniel is not merely mystic, but prophet, too, for he says to Chris: "'You could say that I know it is important for you personally to understand about heaven—about dying—because in only a few years—'" (p. 71). And Chris, horrified at the implied conclusion to Nat's sentence—"'because in only a few years you will be dead'" (p. 72)—rejects Nat for a fool, and finally comes to harbor a secret hatred of his friend, especially after Nat wins Mary Lovell. Ironically, Chris's last order from the bridge, seconds before his ship is struck by the torpedo, is designed to murder Nat, now his shipmate, by throwing him into the sea from his accustomed perch on a rail (pp. 185–86). The guilt Martin feels for this cannot be dispelled by his attempted rationalization: "'And it was the right bloody order!'" (p. 186).[14]

Nat's role in this novel is comparable to those of Simon in *Lord of the Flies* and Tuami in *The Inheritors*. Again Golding points out that the interpreter of truth—whether saint or artist—is often ignored, or misunderstood and maligned, if not actually murdered; and again he points out that this must cause such men to take the utmost care in embodying and communicating their visions. Golding, himself, seems resolved to bring his readers the truth by inviting them to see through eyes other than their own—hence his experimentation with limited points of view, and especially his controversial endings, with their abrupt shifts of focus. The presence of such characters as Simon, Tuami, and Nat in Golding's novels shows that, bleak as man's condition may be, other possibilities exist. And it is in this respect that one must deny, with Golding, Christopher Martin's universality: he represents an extreme position, as does Nat. But Nat's existence illuminates Golding's real point: not a condemnation of modern man, but rather a warning—to the Campbells and the Davidsons, "the type of human intercourse" (p. 207)—to seek out and accept the truths of life and death, as the only way to avoid the egotistical excess that leads Martin to his tangled web of deceit and annihilation.

But *Pincher Martin* does not end with Martin's death. And, unfortunately for Golding, the final sentence of the novel—which establishes beyond doubt that Martin's ordeal on the rock is a postmortem experience—provoked harsh, or at least puzzled, response from numerous early reviewers and critics. Of course, time and more judicious criticism have reestablished the balance of opinion in Golding's favor.[15] However, many critics persist in seeing Martin as a character who confounds his creator's intentions. Peter Green, for example, who admires Golding greatly, observes: "Pincher—like Milton's Satan—breaks away from his creator's original intention. However despicable his character . . . he nevertheless compels our admiring respect for his epic, unyielding struggle in the face of overwhelming odds."[16] Such readings of the novel lend considerable force to Golding's point about modern man. For, although the word *gimmick* can be misleading in a discussion of Golding's methods, it is fairly clear that in *Pincher Martin* his traps are out for the unwary reader. The desire of many readers to see Martin as a heroic figure merely underlines Golding's view that we are far too concerned with survival and not concerned enough with the means by which it is achieved.

Indeed, the same misdirected concern for survival at all costs is precisely what gets in the way of one's perception with regard to Martin's death. Even a cursory rereading of the novel confronts one with myriad clues to Martin's actual situation. Only one such example, the last paragraph of chapter eleven, should suffice:

> His tongue felt along the barrier of his teeth—round to the side where the big ones were and the gap. . . . His tongue was remembering. It pried into the gap between the teeth and created the old, aching shape. It touched the rough edge of the cliff, traced the slope down, trench after aching trench, down towards the smooth surface where the Red Lion was, just above the gum—understood what was

> so hauntingly familiar and painful about an isolated and decaying
> rock in the middle of the sea.   (p. 174)

One is so concerned with survival, so afraid of death, that, like
Martin, he seizes at first on any explanation that will preserve
the protagonist's life or the illusion of life, ignoring any evidence
to the contrary. Truth, in short, becomes abhorrent in preference
to the more palatable self-deception. And Golding's point is
thrust home once again.

The startling immediacy and almost palpable texture of the
physical images in the novel's first three chapters are more than
a little responsible for the reader's reluctance to question the fundamental reality of Martin's projected world (see particularly
the opening paragraph of chapter three, pp. 40–41). Indeed,
one is given little chance even to formulate questions in these
early chapters, narrowed as they are to an almost unceasing bar-
rage of sensation. Martin's ingenuity in relation to his situation
must be noted here (as well as Golding's with relation to the
reader): he confines himself initially to the creation of a limited
world until he has time to develop a more organized vision and
more sophisticated detail. Ironically, the chapters that give Martin time to think inhibit thought on the part of the reader.

As it reveals the power of Golding's language, so *Pincher Martin* reveals a strain of oral-anal imagery so pervasive and unpleasant as to seem almost obsessive. One thinks of the motif of
the maggots and the Chinese box, the bizarre enema scene, the
repulsiveness of much of the imagery, the unrelieved nastiness of
the sexual scenes, and the central metaphor of the island as an
aching tooth, of Martin in a giant mouth about to be swallowed.
One readily concedes that the unpleasantness of language and
symbol is appropriate, even vital, to Martin's character and to
the novel's theme; but one also remembers the cannibalism and
aversion to sexuality of *The Inheritors*, the scatological imagery
and the Oedipal pig-killing of *Lord of the Flies*. All in all, it
would seem that Golding's moral passion, Swiftian in its intensity, seems Swiftian, too, in its association of basic bodily functions with uncleanness and sin.

Golding handles the phantasmagoric scenes in *Pincher Martin*
with great skill, managing to maintain a high level of suspense
by suggesting the delirium of a man under severe strain, while at
the same time offering explicit indication that he is recording the
inexorable breakdown of a desperate illusion. In order to do

this, he weaves together Martin's self-created "present" and the intrusions of flashback and nightmare, as well as several complex symbolic motifs and a host of literary and mythical-religious allusions. It is by any standards a scintillating performance, made the more admirable by the fact that its apparent confusion is underpinned by a rigorously logical foundation.

The more conventional flashback scenes, grounded mainly in dialogue that illuminates Martin's character, may be seen as Golding's main concession to those critics who assailed his eccentric vision as too far removed from the modern world. In these scenes Golding sketches a character from the contemporary milieu, giving him a profession, a circumstantial past, and even an individual psychological makeup. But Golding makes sure that Martin's contemporary milieu and individual characteristics function organically within the larger metaphysical structure of the novel. And though the novel is vitally concerned with modern man, the critical reception of *Pincher Martin* indicates that Golding's concession was hardly viewed as such. And in a sense he makes no concession. The glimpses he affords of Martin's past are sketchy, denying, as Kinkead-Weekes and Gregor observe: "assumptions about 'character' and 'relationships' which we may tend to think of as axiomatic for the novel." [17] And finally, the startling conclusion of *Pincher Martin* seems to distinguish the book as an assertion of Golding's earlier methods, rather than a concession to conventions of the novel. But a subtle shift in the direction of those conventions is nonetheless apparent.

John Peter observes, in comparing *Pincher Martin* with Golding's first two novels, that it is "richer because exploratory, a configuration of symbols rather than an allegory, and for this reason it will bear an intensity of attention that its predecessors could not sustain." [18] Whether or not he might quarrel with Peter's assessment, Golding himself, in the period between publication of *Pincher Martin* and his fourth novel, *Free Fall*, indicated a shift in concern by describing his next project as an attempt to show "the patternlessness of life before we impose our patterns on it." [19] Thus, one may see *Pincher Martin* as a transitional work, both an end and a beginning, and also, in John Peter's words, "as brilliant a conception as any fable in English prose." [20]

5.

Free Fall:
The Prevalence of Pattern

Before the publication in 1959 of *Free Fall*, Golding had described the forthcoming novel as dealing with "the patternlessness of life." Coming from a man whose first three novels had seemed to many critics simplistic in their moral outlook and so tightly controlled and patterned as to approach allegory, this statement appeared to indicate a fundamental change in strategy, if not of vision. And *Free Fall* was strikingly different in a number of ways from Golding's earlier works: in it he again seemed to respond to his critics by dealing with areas of experience that they had accused him of neglecting, and by adopting a form and methods closer to the mainstream of novelistic convention. As in his earlier works, however, Golding had his own aims firmly in mind, and the book is far more than a mere accommodation of the critical appetite for a social novel.

Like its immediate predecessor, *Pincher Martin*, *Free Fall* focuses on an individual: Sammy Mountjoy, a well-known painter. The novel is a first-person account (Golding's first) of Sammy's attempt to discover the point at which he lost his innocence: "the connection between the little boy, clear as spring water, and the man like a stagnant pool."[1] In a sense, the book reads like that most familiar of modern novelistic types, the *Künstlerroman*, for Sammy's story is certainly a portrait of the artist, covering most of the standard crises—from childhood to manhood—in the maturing of a sensitive youth. Sammy, however, makes pointed reference to "those books which kept turning up in the twenties," the heroes of which were "bad at games, unhappy and misunderstood at school—tragic, in fact, until they reached eighteen or nineteen and published a stunning book of poems or took to interior decoration" (p. 48). This passage is an obviously satirical reference—though it misses by a decade—to the two best-known works in the genre, James Joyce's *A Portrait of the Artist as a Young Man* (1916) and D. H. Lawrence's *Sons and Lovers* (1913), as well as to the numerous imitations that followed them. And though Sammy mentions the books in describing another character, the reader may consider the allusion as Golding's invitation to compare his own novel to the type that it ironically parallels. There are numerous incidental and thematic correspondences between *Free Fall* and the two earlier works, but what strikes one most immediately in comparing the novel with those of Joyce and Lawrence is the difference in chronology and, consequently, attitude. Whereas the earlier novels were chronologically linear narratives, mainly concerned with the escape of their protagonists from the maze of the past, Sammy's story is an obliquely chronicled account of its narrator's willing—almost obsessive—return to that maze. The hopeful, or at least unknown, future to which Stephen Dedalus and Paul Morel turn at the close of their stories is for Sammy Mountjoy the painful, disillusioned present; and it is precisely the comparative absence of illusion that separates *Free Fall* from the other two novels.

Should this comparison seem to indicate arrogance on Golding's part, one should remember that the story is Sammy's, not Golding's, and that Golding, who at twenty-one saw a volume of his own youthful poems published, knows well the discomfort of retrospective judgment on such callow productions (see *The Hot Gates*, pp. 26–28). But, again, the facts of Sammy's life—aside from scattered parallels—are not those of Golding's. In *Talk: Conversations with William Golding*, Golding has this to say on the subject: "*Free Fall* was an invention from beginning to end, a deliberate invention. All the terms of my life were turned upside down. . . . I said to myself, 'You were in the navy; well this man has to be in the army. You are a writer; you'll have to make this man a painter.'" But this inverted autobiography in no way diminishes its validity as a record of Golding's intellectual development, as he further observes in *Talk*:

> The particular poignancy of the model intellectual of the twentieth century—which is what we most of us are, unless we have committed ourselves to something; in which case, we're lucky—the poignancy of the model intellectual is that he is literally in a state of free fall. . . .

Where for hundreds of thousands of years men have known where they were, now they don't know where they are any longer. This is the point of *Free Fall*.[2]

In his first three novels Golding examined, from different angles and with differing emphases, the essential proposition that man's rational, creative powers may be applied with devastating effect to ways of avoiding, as well as pursuing, truth. In *Lord of the Flies* Golding deals mainly with the consequences of that proposition, showing the destruction that may be unleashed when man turns from the fact of his own nature. Both groups of boys on the island, civilized and savage, are living by elaborated myths, neither of which confronts the duality of human nature. In *The Inheritors* the proposition is examined in more detail, comprehending not only consequences, but also first causes, culminating in the moment when Tuami perceives that the potential for creation and destruction, order and disorder, lives within man, implying that the urge to survive is supported by an intellect that may delude as well as save. *Pincher Martin* is an exhaustive demonstration of the original proposition, dramatically illustrating the delusive and egotistical lengths to which man's creative powers may take him in the name of survival.

Central to Golding's views as embodied in those first three novels was his reaction against rationalism, which attempted to ignore the darkness and irrationality that existed for him even in childhood (*The Hot Gates*, pp. 168–70). And his childish intuitions of a darker side to nature are the wellsprings of the theme that runs throughout his work. The young Golding, unable to articulate his fears in the face of his father's calm rationalism, foreshadowed the mystical characters in his own novels—Simon, Tuami, Nathaniel—all of whom experience difficulty—perhaps too mild a word—in communicating their insights. Their plight parallels that of many who deal in the stuff of vision and intuition, whether martyred saints or misunderstood artists. And Golding's concern for this dual aspect—aesthetic and religious—of the perception and communication of truth increases from novel to novel. If in *Lord of the Flies* Golding presents his readers with a fait accompli, a comparatively finished—even didactic—vision of the truth, his two subsequent novels steadily qualify and reexamine that vision, seeming almost to antedate its philosophical stance in an attempt to explain it and lend it greater authority.

Free Fall is a kind of reverse *Pincher Martin* in that the protagonist brings his intelligence and creativity to bear on the task of finding, rather than avoiding, the truth. Sammy Mountjoy is ultimately like a fusion of Christopher Martin and Nathaniel Walterson: with a past as sinful as Martin's, Sammy is nonetheless a true artist where Chris is a parody; and with Nathaniel's passion for truth, Sammy, unlike the awkward saint, possesses communicative gifts of a rather high order. Sammy, as an artist, is the first character whom Golding allows relatively complete use of both rational and intuitive powers, underlining sharply the degree to which point of view is limited in the preceding novels, and indicating the fulness of Golding's commitment to a thorough examination of his subject. And, as a further earnest of his objectivity, Golding offers a protagonist who purports to have small hope for the enlightenment to be derived from form; unlike Pincher Martin, Sammy Mountjoy aspires to find, not to impose, pattern. He realizes the difficulties of his task: "The mind cannot hold more than so much; but understanding requires a sweep that takes in the whole of remembered time and then can pause" (p. 7). And he accepts its obsessive, frustrated nature—"To communicate is our passion and our despair" (p. 8). Thus, his hopes are modest:

> I may communicate in part; and that surely is better than utter blind and dumb. . . . Not that I aspire to complete coherence. Our mistake is to confuse our limitations with the bounds of possibility and clap the universe into a rationalist hat or some other. But I may find the indications of a pattern that will include me, even if the outer edges tail off into ignorance.   (p. 9)

Despite the indication of antirationalism in the above quotation, one must beware of drawing hasty conclusions. Perhaps somewhat self-conscious of the extent to which the antirationalist bias had marked his previous works, Golding expends a good deal of effort on balancing his protagonist's views on the subject; for Sammy, rationalism is not a special target, but rather one of a number of systems that he has "hung . . . on the wall like a row of useless hats" (p. 6). And Sammy's step-by-step examination of his past causes him to reconsider each of his "hats," so that *Free Fall* is the first novel in which Golding offers anything like a comprehensive view of the various ways that man has evolved of regarding and dealing with his universe. As Frank Kermode says, "*Free Fall* . . . is about everything."[3] And the attempt to be comprehensive necessarily leads the novel beyond the closer strictures of Golding's earlier work, moving it farther from the mode of fable and closer to that of fiction, which John Peter has described as "a more or less faithful reflection of the complexities, and often of the irrelevancies, of life as it is actually experienced."[4] Whether this description may ultimately be applied to *Free Fall* is worth considering, though the evidence makes the judgment difficult.

The question of viewpoint, for example, is a complicating factor. Sammy is a first-person narrator; and though he may, for the most part, reflect Golding's own intellectual preoccupations and beliefs, Golding, as author, is finally at a remove from his character. Though Sammy's review of his past may be puzzled and desperate, the steps in that exploration and the events of his life—past and present—are under Golding's firm control. Thus, one must evaluate *Free Fall* as a double-edged dramatization of the difficulties of perceiving and communicating truth: the story is Sammy's, but the novel is Golding's; one must judge both. Sammy's account may be true to his life, but is Golding's novel true to ours? Adding to the difficulty is the fact that both Sammy and Golding are self-conscious artists: both know the almost obsessive power of apocalyptic vision, vision so compelling as to control the creator's hand, to make the substantiating pattern appear. Sammy, indeed, begins his story with an acknowledgment of such vision, and of the compulsion to reexamine it:

> I have walked by stalls in the market-place where books, dog-eared and faded from their purple, have burst with a white hosanna. I have seen people crowned with a double crown, holding in either hand the crook and flail, the power and the glory. I have understood how the scar becomes a star, I have felt the flake of fire fall, miraculous and pentecostal. My yesterdays walk with me. They keep step, they are grey faces that peer over my shoulder. I live on Paradise Hill, ten minutes from the station, thirty seconds from the shops and the local. Yet I am a burning amateur, torn by the irrational and incoherent, violently searching and self-condemned.   (p. 1)

Hence Sammy's story, and Golding's novel—perhaps his career. A major factor in the apocalyptic, visionary quality of Golding's first three novels is their deliberate, microcosmic isolation from the larger sphere of human life and preoccupation with the elemental problem of survival. *Pincher Martin*, Golding's first attempt to deal with contemporary man, is nonetheless dominated by the motifs of survival and isolation; even in his social behavior, Martin is influenced and isolated from his fellows by his perversely sublimated survival urge. In *Free Fall*, as Golding moves more completely into the social arena, the survival motif recedes; the theme of isolation remains, at first mainly apparent in the familiar literary treatment of the individual's isolation within society.

In one crucial episode, however, Golding returns to the dramatic and visionary technique of his previous novels. This section reveals why Sammy has undertaken his self-examination and how he "acquired or was given the capacity to see" (p. 133). The setting is a German POW camp during World War II, where Sammy is being interrogated by a Gestapo psychologist, Dr. Halde, concerning his knowledge of escape plans. As a kind of torture, Halde has Sammy locked in a dark cell (which, unknown to Sammy, is merely a broom closet); and here, driven almost mad by his childhood-rooted fear of the dark, Sammy paradoxically acquires the vision and the compulsion to search for the source of his guilt. The prison camp ordeal, with its emphasis on physical isolation as a forcing-bed of revelation and discovery, reminds one dramatically of the earlier Golding, especially of *Pincher Martin*, even to Martin's fear of the dark. This time, however, the protagonist emerges from his isolation to live again. But as with Ralph in *Lord of the Flies*, Sammy's "rescue" is merely physical—the inner torture goes on as a function of life.

The reader must wait, however, until near the halfway point of the novel to learn of Sammy's transfiguring experience, since his distrust for the rational mode of cause and effect controls the very form of his narrative. "For time," he writes,

> is not to be laid out endlessly like a row of bricks. That straight line from the first hiccup to the last gasp is a dead thing. Time is two modes. The one is an effortless perception native to us as water to the mackerel. The other is a memory, a sense of shuffle fold and coil, of that day nearer than that because more important, of that event mirroring this, or those three set apart, exceptional and out of the straight line altogether.   (p. 6)

Of Earth and Darkness

But in choosing narrative obliquity over mere chronology, Sammy is simply replacing one kind of pattern with another. And while his imaginative sense of "shuffle fold and coil" may bring life to his story, his main purpose—to understand how the boy became the man—nonetheless exerts its pressure in favor of straight-line reasoning. And here is the paradox that tugs the novel this way and that: that the telling may compromise the truth of the tale. But the motivating force remains: the compulsion of the artist to create, of the visionary to communicate.

The particular sin that most haunts Sammy is his youthful seduction and subsequent abandonment of a girl, Beatrice Ifor. Compounding his guilt is the fact that shortly after he had abandoned her (although he does not learn of it until much later), Beatrice had suffered an irreversible mental collapse. But Sammy is concerned with more than the particulars of his sins, however great, however haunting. His goal is to isolate the moment at which he made the step from the freedom of innocence to the captivity of guilt, to recognize, as he says, "the decision made freely that cost me my freedom" (p. 7). Thus, he begins his search with an examination of his early childhood.

Lord of the Flies attempts to "trace the defects of society back to the defects of human nature." No less a study of human guilt, *Free Fall* nevertheless appears to modify that view somewhat. Sammy's description of his childhood—the first three chapters of the novel—makes a persuasive case for the influence on the individual of various agents, social, cultural, and personal.

Bastard child of an unknown father, Sammy spends his earliest years in the slums of Rotten Row under two dominant influences: that of his Ma, "as near a whore as makes no matter," who nonetheless represents in her hugeness and matter-of-factness perhaps the one constant in a chaotic world; and Evie, who may have been "a congenital liar," but whose flair for fantasy helps to brighten Sammy's childish world (p. 33). In these two may be seen the seeds of Sammy's art itself. Speaking of Ma's guessed-at sexual life, he observes: "Her casual intercourse must have been to her what his works are to a real artist—themselves and nothing more. They had no implication" (p. 15). But again the paradox, again the tension, for the child Sammy sees in Evie the value of a vision that transmutes Ma's matter-of-fact reality by responding to its implications, and of the satisfaction, even the joy, of communication.

Looking back, Sammy finds Rotten Row "roaring and warm, simple and complex, individual and strangely happy and a world unto itself" (p. 33). His life there is free from sin. But one can see in this section other events that play a part in his later life. The death one night of Ma's lodger, which rouses Sammy from sleep to waking nightmare, lays the foundation for the fear of the dark that triggers his moral awakening. And when Minnie, a retarded schoolmate, responds to a school inspector's questions by urinating in terror on the floor, Sammy, like the other children, is "exalted" with a sense of his own humanity, foreshadowing a later episode that brings him to a state far removed from exaltation.

Sammy next examines his boyhood to see if the stain of sin may be isolated there. He describes, and discards as innocent, two incidents involving him and a daredevil friend, Johnny Spragg. Both events are minor acts of trespass: first, the boys sneak onto an airfield to see the results of a plane crash; then they venture onto the grounds of "the general's house," a huge mansion on Paradise Hill, overlooking Rotten Row. Each incident, however, carries its subtle warning for Sammy. At the airport, out of the mist that had caused the crash, and against the background smoke and flames from the wreckage, a man appears "from nowhere . . . tall and hatless and smeared with black" (p. 41), to chase the boys off. Trespassing on the general's grounds, the boys from Rotten Row are "two points of perception, wandering in paradise" (p. 45). Preceded by a kind of pagan innocence in the world of Ma and Evie, Sammy's experiences with "the god on the airfield" and at the general's house are like glimpses of hell and heaven for one unacquainted with their theology. The schematics of these paired scenes may cause one to reflect on the obtuseness of Sammy's remarks on them: "They contributed very little to the straight line of my story. . . . But they are not important in that way. They are important simply because they emerge" (p. 46). Above all, one may wonder at Golding's disingenuousness in putting such remarks in Sammy's story, especially since the general's mansion appears later in the novel as the hospital in which Beatrice is confined.

Sammy's search proceeds to another pair of incidents, this time involving Philip Arnold, a sly boy who "knew about people" (p. 49) enough to use their weaknesses to his own advantage. Philip persuades the stronger Sammy to extort from younger children the "fagcards" that Sammy loves because of their pictures of the kings of Egypt, whose "austere and proud faces" reflect what he "felt people should be" (p. 50). When this scheme fails, not without introducing Sammy to guilt, Philip next persuades him to desecrate the altar of a local church. This plan, too, is exploded at the crucial moment by the verger, who strikes Sammy on the ear, causing him eventually to be hospitalized with a mastoid condition. This incident, and a teacher whose interpretation of the Gospel is punctuated by smacks, provide Sammy with a less than endearing introduction to formal religion. Sammy's Ma dies while he is hospitalized, and when he is adopted by the priest whose church he had attempted to desecrate, the boy is paradoxically lost to religious influence; for Father Watts-Watt (whose very name suggests bewilderment) is ineffectual, paranoid, and torn by homosexual desires. Thus, fearing contact with Sammy, Watts-Watt remains distant, his major influence upon his ward being to increase the boy's fear of the dark (see chapter eight). And though Sammy concedes that Philip had altered his life, he nevertheless sees himself at the end of his childhood as "innocent of guilt, unconscious of innocence" (p. 78).

Sammy now jumps in time, for the next three chapters (four through six), to consider his affair with Beatrice. And in this section, much of the novel's underlying symbolism becomes clear. These chapters comprise, too, an altered, but recognizably elaborated version of the Chris Martin-Mary Lovell relationship in *Pincher Martin*. This sequence may be seen as Golding's answer to those critics who had bemoaned the absence of sexual relationships in his fiction. Indeed, Golding gives the Sammy-Beatrice affair a complex and circumstantial treatment that seems to ground *Free Fall* more firmly in the fictional mode, and develops further the motif of social determinism created by the childhood episodes. And the account of Sammy's adolescent yearnings for the naive and inhibited girl is at first so familiar a story as to seem humorous (which it often is). Golding skillfully blends high-flown romantic sentiments and frequently embarrassing—even tasteless—details that make his depiction of adolescent love at once convincing for the reader and painful for the retrospective narrator. Sammy's lack of freedom here seems at first merely a function of his status as young man in love.

But something darker lies beneath the surface. The naive Sammy, who has joined the Communist party because its members "know where [they] are going" (pp. 88–90), is driven by deeper and more dangerous currents. His understandable desire to communicate with Beatrice seems obsessively metaphysical, as well as sexual:

> "I want you, I want all of you, not just cold kisses and walks—I want to be with you and in you and on you and round you—I want fusion and identity—I want to understand and be understood—oh God, Beatrice, Beatrice, I love you—I want to be you!"   (p. 105)

One begins to see that this entire section of the novel is Sammy's *Vita Nuova*, that Golding's symbolic bent is asserting itself forcefully in a modern parody of Dante's works. Sammy first sees his Beatrice as a model in a drawing class, posed before a pictured Palladian bridge. He meets her "accidentally" by crossing another bridge at the beginning of their affair. Initially, too, she is as unattainable as Dante's Beatrice, and as much an embodiment of perfect Being.

But Sammy, failing to trust, as Dante did, the artist in him, is driven to possess Beatrice physically; upon achieving that possession, he finds that the proof of the symbol is not in the flesh. Beatrice is rendered "impotent" by "the weight of her half-baked sectarianism" (p. 120).[5] And ironically, Sammy's art comes closer to the understanding he seeks than his frantic attempts to communicate with her through sexual exploitation. Instead of catching the terror of her exploitation, as he had intended, his most striking picture exalts her, revealing the real peace and perfection that his physical assaults have failed to reach (pp. 123–24). But those assaults take their toll of Sammy. As he says on looking back: "They reinforced the reality of physical life and they destroyed the possibility of anything else; and they made physical life not only three times real but contemptible. And under everything else, deep, was an anguish of helplessness and loss" (p. 123).

So Sammy runs madly, after two agonizing years, away from

his now-intolerable affair, from the knowledge that divine love cannot exist for him. Somewhere between Lawrence's Paul Morel, who rejects the inhibited Miriam but cannot find peace with the "liberated" Clara Dawes, and Joyce's Stephen Dedalus, who consciously follows Dante's example in renouncing "E. C." for art's sake, Sammy finds in Taffy—whom he meets through the Party—the woman he needs, sensually, psychologically, and intellectually. Beatrice, like the Party, is left behind, diminished—and note the irony here—to a mere "skeleton in the cupboard" (p. 128). Is this the point for which Sammy is searching? "What else could I have done," he says, "but run away from Beatrice? . . . I had lost my power to choose" (pp. 130–31).

But if during the Beatrice affair Sammy has already lost his freedom, knowledge of that loss comes soon after, with the war. And now the older Sammy focuses on his experience in the prison camp, as if to prepare himself and the reader for the doubling-back to the adolescent period that must hold his moment of decision. One must note, too, that the camp scenes are strategically placed in Golding's symbolic scheme: if the preceding three chapters have been Sammy's *Vita Nuova*, placement of the camp scenes at this point insures linear development of the novel's Dantean parallel from *Inferno* (chapter nine) through *Purgatorio* (ten) and *Paradiso* (thirteen). And there is more: in chapter seven, Halde's interrogation of Sammy becomes an ironic version of the temptation of Christ (pp. 146–47), as Golding continues to allude—as in the childhood scenes—to the Old and New Testaments, strengthening the ethical-religious implications of Sammy's role.

Sammy, no hero, is willing but unable to yield to Halde's temptations. Such knowledge as he possesses about his fellow prisoners is, like his artist's vision, intuitive, not factual, and means nothing in Halde's rational world. Thus, he is locked in the cell and undergoes an ordeal that, rather than extracting knowledge from him, gives it to him. And here there is another jump in time, as Sammy returns (in chapter eight) to his childhood, attempting to trace his fear of the dark to his life with Father Watts-Watt. The examination fails in its stated purpose, but the chapter is notable for further symbolic references in which Sammy is linked with Daedalus or Icarus (pp. 154–55) and Prometheus (pp. 157–58); the rectory itself is like a labyrinth, Christian rather than pagan. Unlike Joyce's Stephen, however, who escapes from the labyrinthine streets of Catholic Dublin, Sammy must wait until his imprisonment by Halde to realize that his true labyrinth, like pagan Daedalus's, is self-created, and like his Dantesque inferno, exists within himself.

Locked in the closet-cell, Sammy's concern for his "privates" (p. 166) underlines the extent to which sex has become central in his life, and causes him to imagine that a forgotten floor-cloth, lying damply before him, is a severed penis, focus of his fears. This is Sammy's *Inferno*, and Golding's prose now creates a sense of darkness and unmanageable fear that is almost palpable. But at the moment of crisis, when all hope seems lost, Sammy utters a cry for help. And at this point one is reminded again of Pincher Martin, who could not cry for help. Drowning, like Martin, in a "sea of nightmare," Sammy finds no hope of help, either in the physical world or in his own memory; unlike Martin, however, Sammy faces the unknown future, ready to die (pp. 184–85).

Instead of death, Sammy is given life. His cries are answered by the camp commandant, who releases him from physical torture; but Sammy has already been resurrected by his decision to face the truth. Thus, in his *Purgatorio* (chapter ten), Sammy wanders through the camp seeing life anew, seeing a world where all things shine "with the innocent light of their own created nature" (p. 186). He is "visited by a flake of fire, miraculous and pentecostal; . . . transmuted . . . once and forever" (p. 188). As with Moses, the veil has been lifted from Sammy's eyes, and like his biblical namesake, Samuel, he is enabled to perceive the qualities of kingship. Paradoxically he finds these qualities in all men, able at last to see the connection between the kings of Egypt and humanity at large. His sketches of his fellow prisoners are transformed by his new perception into the images of those kings, becoming, as he says, "the glory of my right hand" (p. 188). He perceives, too, that each man must be kingly, since he and his fellows are the "pillars" upon which order rests. Thus, though man is influenced, even changed, by everything around him, as *Free Fall* concedes, the burden of individual responsibility remains—the "kingdom" cannot be given away.

Conscious, then, of the responsibilities of kingship, Sammy examines his own nature, and finds himself lacking. He finds his inner being "loathsome and abject," and the unendurable discovery drives him to search for the point at which he became so (pp. 190–91). In doing so he reminds one again of his biblical counterpart: like that early Samuel, no king himself, he becomes a prophet who can reveal the requisites of kingship and choose the man for the job. And Sammy's choice for king is all men, a prophecy burdensome, but indisputably valid.

Sammy's purgatorial search leads him to his latter schooldays, where—again in Dantesque terms—he is torn between the World of the Spirit and the World of the Flesh, paradoxically personified in Rowena Pringle, the fanatically religious spinster form-mistress and teacher of Scripture, and Nick Shales, the gentle rationalist and science instructor. Repelled by Miss Pringle's vindictiveness—she sees Sammy as an obstacle to her frustrated love of Watts-Watt—and attracted by Nick's gentleness, Sammy—"the earnest metaphysical boy"—slams the door shut "on Moses and Jehovah" and chooses the world of rationalism (pp. 204, 217). This choice, powerfully influenced by outside forces, cannot be the source of Sammy's guilt. But when Sammy's sexual nature is awakened, he finds in Nick's rationalism a haven of realitivistic morality. And though his first glimpse of Beatrice momentarily rekindles his belief in "the beauty of holiness" (p. 226), the powerful physical drive is too strong for his weakened faith. In a scene once more reminiscent of Joyce, Sammy wanders, at the end of his schooldays, in the woods by the river, and experiences, like Stephen Dedalus, a vision of his destiny (pp. 235–36).[6] But while Stephen's experience is mystical, turning him away from the wading girl and the swimmers to art, Sammy's is sensual: he himself becomes a swimmer, and turns from art to his desire for Beatrice. And here, in his decision to sacrifice "everything" to possess Beatrice, Sammy comes closest to isolating the moment of his fall.

But Sammy's story—and Golding's novel—does not end here. The *Paradiso* remains. Like Dante, Sammy attains Paradise Hill. But not until he visits Beatrice, now confined in "the general's house," does he experience the full irony of his position. At the gate house, as Dantean reminders, are three stuffed animals— the lion of pride, the serpent of seduction, and the goat of lechery—emblems of Sammy's sin (p. 237). And "up to the neck in ice" (p. 241) like the sinners at the center of hell, Sammy is confronted by Beatrice.[7] Here, the Dantean echoes are particularly bitter, combining *Paradiso* and *La Vita Nuova*: nine years after their first meeting Dante had again seen Beatrice, whose ineffable salute brought him to the heights of beatitude; nine years after the beginning of their affair, Sammy's Beatrice also salutes him in a sickening parody that recalls from his childhood the "disgrace" of Minnie. This time, however, the disgrace is Sammy's, and he realizes that the World of the Flesh and the World of the Spirit "exist side by side. They meet in me. We have to satisfy the examiners in both worlds at once" (p. 244).

In the novel's final chapter, Sammy attempts to communicate his insights to his "spiritual parents," Nick and Rowena, attempts to explain that the wicked (like Philip Arnold, now a "minister of the crown") and the innocent (like Nick and Beatrice) can live in one world, while the guilty (like himself and Rowena) must live in both. But he finds Nick dying, far beyond the reach of his explanations; even more shaking, he finds that Rowena has succeeded in deluding herself that she is innocent and is now "living in only one world" (p. 252). Thus, confounded in his attempts at explanation, Sammy concludes that his larger quest for a pattern that will include him has failed, that while both worlds are real, "there is no bridge" (p. 253). This conclusion truly leaves him "falling free" between two worlds.

At this point, in the style of his previous novels, Golding causes Sammy to append a clarifying postscript to his story. Appropriately, this involves a return to the scene of Sammy's awakening, when the German commandant releases him from the cell. In ludicrous stage-German, the commandant pronounces the novel's final words: " 'The Herr Doctor does not know about peoples' " (p. 253). This apology to Sammy for Halde's cruelty seems simple enough, seems, indeed, to reiterate the point that Sammy has just made: that those who presume to explain the universe (whether Halde, or Philip Arnold, or Sammy, or Golding himself) are doomed to delusion, since explanations and patterns are reductive. But Sammy regards the words as "inscrutable," to be puzzled over "as though they were the Sphinx's riddle" (p. 253). And here, in the reference to the Sphinx's riddle, is the key to Golding's final, paradoxical comment on both Sammy's story and his own novel. For the answer to the

Of Earth and Darkness

Sphinx's riddle is "man." And man is likewise the answer to
Sammy's riddle, and to Golding's: man's limitations insure his
inability to understand and explain all, but man is the very real
bridge between his own attempts at explanation. Thus, in a
sense, Sammy's vision and Golding's are both right and wrong,
for man will continue to make leaps of faith and attempt explanations: it is in his nature.

For all its incorporation of naturalistic techniques, *Free Fall* is
at least as intricately patterned as Golding's earlier works.
Drawing on a reservoir of allusion that includes classical, biblical, medieval, and contemporary sources, Golding attempts—
exceeding at least in volume the allusive efforts of Joyce and
Lawrence—to give mythical dimensions to his portrait of the
artist.[8] Choosing Dante as the artistic ideal, Golding shows how
a Sammy or a Paul Morel or a Stephen Dedalus or a Golding
may aspire to such status, aspire to mirror and comprehend both
the degradation and mystical beauty of the universe. But he
shows, too, how modern man's conscious separation of the two
worlds makes difficult such a fusion of Daedalus, the artificer,
and Prometheus, the bringer of light, of Aaron, the speaker, and
Moses, the seer. Golding's Sammy, presumably like his creator,
is an incomplete fusion of the two artistic elements. Thus,
Sammy's story and Golding's novel reflect the central dilemma
of modern art, in which visionary and naturalistic elements are
seldom united as effectively as by Joyce and Lawrence.

Golding's own apparent concessions to the techniques of
naturalism and the concept of social determinism seem finally,
like the concessions of *Pincher Martin*, mainly functional, designed to throw into sharper outline the contrast between past
and present. And even the particulars of Sammy's story, puzzling
as they may be to him, bear the clear marks of Golding's hand.
Sammy's life overflows with clearly patterned foreshadowings,
repetitions for emphasis, and sharply delineated crucial episodes. And underlying or impressed on every segment is the
dualistic structure that influences Sammy's ultimate vision: at
every point in the story, Sammy revolves between two outside
influences—Ma and Evie, Johnny and Philip, Alsopp and Wim-
bury (of the Party), Beatrice and Taffy, Halde and the commandant, Nick and Rowena, and so forth. And the characterization
is often sketchy, even to the point of triteness, as with Nick and

Rowena, who are common literary types whose presence in the story seems almost wholly functional. Functional, too, are the actual events of the novel; nothing is wasted, nothing irrelevant introduced, each incident cleaving to the main purpose. Even the language observes the pervasive pattern of duality: flat narrative acting as connector between apocalyptic, often grandiose, flights and the unpleasant, cloacal imagery of sin that runs like an open sewer through Golding's works.

One may qualify these observations by noting again that the story is Sammy's, and his is the selecting hand, but this is really to beg the question. One may add, too, that *Free Fall* does represent an extension of Golding's range in its contemporaneity, its fuller treatment of human relationships, and its acknowledgment of sociocultural influences on the individual. But one cannot finally agree that *Free Fall* is fully realized fiction of the kind described by John Peter, especially with respect to portraying life's "irrelevancies." As Kinkead-Weekes and Gregor point out, Golding's art in *Free Fall* is "capable of dealing with new complexities in a new way; but it never wholly commits itself to that way without revealing a clear tendency to veer back."[9]

The difficulties of *Free Fall* arise in part from a conceptual flaw: the self-conscious, retrospective narrative robs Sammy's discoveries of much of their potential dramatic impact and causes a cerebral selection of detail that—however vivid—often makes the characters and events seem contrived and merely functional, vitiating Golding's final attempt to suggest the complex nature of man and the universe.[10] Golding clearly identifies Sammy's search with his own intellectual struggles as artist, often seeming to merge with his protagonist, never wholly detached from him. Perhaps as a result, the novel's strategy seems ambiguous, full of self-consciously thematic discourse, unlike that of its predecessors, which are marked by Golding's distance from their characters, a distance that allows him to devote his powers more fully to the dramatization of their struggles.

Most critics of *Free Fall* have found the novel puzzling and irritating; even those, like Kinkead-Weekes and Gregor, who have defended it stoutly, see it as less than a complete success in its efforts to comprehend the disjunctive elements of pattern and chaos.[11] In a sense, however, success or failure is not the main issue: for Golding, *Free Fall* seemed to be a necessary project, an attempt to understand not only the limitations of his own art, but also of human understanding; or in Virginia Tiger's words, "a confession of failure and a confession of growth."[12] In facing his limitations, in facing the prevalence of pattern and the challenge of chaos, Golding may well have achieved the more unified philosophical and artistic vision that produced *The Spire*.

6.

The Spire:
Form and Substance

In 1965, a year after the appearance of *The Spire*, Golding made the following observation in an article for *Holiday* magazine: "For what is a work of art? Is it the form or the substance? 'Both,' we feel, when we think about it at all, 'but if we must choose, give us the substance.'"[1] Reflecting the continued modification in Golding's approach to his art that I have traced through his first four novels, this passage—in an essay on cathedrals—is admirably suited as a gloss on his fifth. *The Spire* seems a culmination of Golding's attempts to unite in a single vision the duality that accounts for much of the tension in his previous novels, a tension that threatened to tear *Free Fall* apart. With the experience of *Free Fall* behind him, Golding nonetheless required almost five years of further thought and creative struggle before resolving that tension in *The Spire*.

The novel is a thinly disguised fictional account of the building of Salisbury Cathedral's four-hundred-foot spire in the thirteenth century. Golding has long made his home in Salisbury, within sight of the spire, and the fictional setting of the novel is Barchester, the pseudonymous Salisbury created by Trollope.[2] That *The Spire* parallels rather closely the architectural and human history of Salisbury Cathedral is perhaps less important than the physical existence of the Salisbury spire. One of the world's architectural marvels, it is at once a testimony to human ingenuity, frailty, and faith, and in this paradoxical compound is the core of Golding's novel. Jocelin, dean of the fictional cathedral and driving force behind construction of the spire, is perhaps the final step in Golding's exploration of the artist-mystic, of the related problems of vision and delusion, creation and communication—indeed, of his own approach to fiction. In Jocelin, Golding unites the various traits of the artist-mystic that appear in simpler form in the earlier works, from Simon, Tuami, and Nat to Christopher Martin and Sammy Mountjoy.

The Spire brings together the concerns of both *Pincher Martin*, which examines man's attempts to impose reductive patterns on the universe, and *Free Fall*, which examines his attempts to confront and communicate its complexity. Jocelin's story, like a large part of Sammy Mountjoy's, is a series of events connecting two visions, with both men passing from pridefully narrow vision to humble recognition of the world's complexity, their own limitations, and their past sins. Sammy's first vision involves the physical world, his second the spiritual (*Free Fall*, pp. 235–36, 184–92); Jocelin's visions reverse that order (*The Spire*, pp. 183–90, 214–15). But for each man the result is the same: the attainment of greater insight and humility at the price of guilt. Both men vow to sacrifice "everything"—and, indeed, the cost is great—to fulfill the promise of their first visions, Sammy opting for possession of Beatrice and Jocelin for creation of the spire. But like Christopher Martin, who is plagued by constant reminders of his death long before he finally succumbs to reality, neither Sammy nor Jocelin can wholly suppress recognition of the "other worlds." Sammy's artistic sense—his unconscious desire for truth—sees the "holy light" in Beatrice that his sensual desires attempt to obscure; and Jocelin's mysticism—also in pursuit, however narrowly, of truth—cannot wholly resist the impingements of the physical world.

Like Martin, but unlike Sammy, Jocelin dies shortly after his realization of the truth. But Jocelin's recognition of the truth is fuller than Martin's and, if not fuller, more dramatically successful than Sammy's. Indeed, the motif of tragic self-discovery present in all of Golding's novels finds its most satisfactory—certainly most classical—dramatization in *The Spire*. The self-knowledge given to Ralph in *Lord of the Flies* and Lok in *The Inheritors* seems pathetic, rather than tragic, because of their limited perception; Tuami's moment of recognition in *The Inheritors* is too brief for tragic force; Chris Martin, for all the intensity of his ordeal, is denied full tragic stature by the blackness of his character, the irony of his posturing, and his final retreat to primal instinct; the story of Sammy Mountjoy, which comes closer to tragic dimensions, is vitiated by Sammy's ultimate bewilderment and by the disjointed, retrospective narrative form. Jocelin, though, emerges, in the words of James Baker, as "a tragic hero in the Euripidean tradition."[3] His story is dramatically tragic in the classical sense, almost a model of Aristotelian structure: he moves inevitably in ordered stages from prideful eminence to reversal and discovery, the whole action arising from his essentially admirable, yet flawed, nature, and dramatized through human interaction.

Jocelin's self-discovery is gradual, and *The Spire*, like all of Golding's novels from *The Inheritors* through *The Pyramid*, employs a limited viewpoint that forces the reader to share in the process, to see first with the protagonist's eyes before becoming a detached observer of the story's ironies and complexities. In *The Inheritors* one shares the perceptions of an awakening primitive intelligence; in *Pincher Martin* the desperate self-deception of a dying man; in *Free Fall* the frustrations and revelations of an artist in search of meaning. In *The Spire* one again sees the world through a narrow but ever-widening vision, this time that of an obsessed artist-mystic whose single-minded dedication to his creation at first blinds him to its complex reality. A measure of Golding's genius is that the process of discovery remains fresh from novel to novel, embodied in newly striking dramatic entities and situations and enhanced by technical virtuosity.

The first chapter of *The Spire* embraces and foreshadows almost all of the novel's themes and plot developments. Like *Free Fall*, the book opens with a passage of highly wrought imagery that serves at once to characterize the oblique angle of its protagonist's vision and to underline Golding's major theme:

> He was laughing, chin up, and shaking his head. God the Father was exploding in his face with a glory of sunlight through painted glass, a glory that moved with his movements to consume and exalt Abraham and Isaac and then God again. The tears of laughter in his eyes made additional spokes and wheels and rainbows.[4]

Here is Jocelin's expression of joy as work on the spire begins. But more important, here is his habitual distinction between the world of God (the spirit) and that of Abraham and Isaac (the flesh). As construction of the spire progresses, Jocelin is forced, like Sammy Mountjoy, to acknowledge that the two worlds cannot be separated, that they are in fact conjoined in his own being; and he learns of his own pride, how he has attempted to take upon himself not only the roles of Isaac (the sacrificial victim) and of Abraham (the visionary), but also that of God (the creator). He comes to recognize that his sacrifices of himself and others have been at best only partially to the glory of God, that he has in his usurpation of God's role attempted to build to his own greater glory, and that he has been motivated, too, by his fleshly nature, by a sublimated desire for Goody Pangall, red-haired wife of the cathedral caretaker.

One perceives almost immediately the novel's sexual dimension, as Jocelin regards a model of the projected building:

> The model was like a man lying on his back. The nave was his legs placed together, the transepts on either side were his arms outspread. The Choir was his body; and the Lady Chapel . . . was his head. And now also, springing, projecting, bursting, erupting from the heart of the building, there was its crown and majesty, the new spire. (p. 4)

Golding's use of a symbol that has become a cliché is a fresh reminder of his responsiveness to technical challenge and, ultimately, a further proof of his skilled craftsmanship. Jocelin, at this early stage, is blind to the sexual implications of his vision, blinded by his spiritual zeal, his distaste for the physical world, his pride. These traits are soon evidenced as he is struck by the apparent solidity of the various "rods and trunks" of light shining through the cathedral's windows, and the "pillar" of light, "straight as Abel's," lifting through the hole in the roof that the workmen have cut to accommodate the spire. Reflecting on this phenomenon, he smiles "to think how the mind touches all things with law, yet deceives itself as easily as a child" (p. 6). Jocelin's complacent and prideful reflection is ironic, since he is revealed by the novel to be a tragic example of just such self-deception.

Jocelin is a would-be allegorist whose work might well be compared to his creator's: his initial conception of the spire as "a diagram of the highest prayer of all" (p. 115) is akin to the simple premises that often underlie Golding's works; and as Golding so often "transcends his programme" to create more than mere fables, Jocelin, too, finds that his creation teaches him "a new lesson at every level" (p. 103). Sammy Mountjoy observes that "art is partly communication, but only partly. The rest is discovery" (*Free Fall*, p. 102). Both *Free Fall* and *The*

Spire are Golding's attempts to demonstrate Sammy's observation. That *The Spire* succeeds while *Free Fall* falters is partially traceable to the fact that in *The Spire* Golding returns to the authorial detachment of his first three novels, creating in Jocelin a foil like Christopher Martin, rather than a confusing sometime alter ego like Sammy. Vital, too, in *The Spire* is Golding's decision to challenge boldly the formal tendency of his own vision. In order to dramatize Jocelin's forced acknowledgement of a complex physical world, Golding must create such a world. Thus, for the first time in his career, Golding is concerned with asserting the primacy of substance over form.

And the world that Jocelin attempts to ignore, or to simplify in conformity with his vision, is indeed substantial and various: Golding's known ability to describe the physical world is fully apparent in *The Spire*, matching the minute tactility of *Pincher Martin* and creating an even more impressive sense of the broader landscape than in *Lord of the Flies* and *The Inheritors*. Accompanying the customarily excellent prose is a new deepening of characterization, a wider range of human relationships, and a sense of the world at large, giving *The Spire* claim to the social dimension that seems lacking in Golding's previous novels. As Jocelin's frequent ascents of the ever-growing spire force him to expand the narrow confines of his vision, so must Golding move—as he attempted to do in *Free Fall*—beyond the stark economy of his earlier works.

Jocelin is continually reminded of the physical world—by the dust, dirt, and noise of construction, by the mud, rain, and fecundity of spring, by the people around him, by his own tormented desires and his tubercular spine, and by the perilous weakness of the spire's foundations. The novel's first four chapters are earthbound, documenting Jocelin's intensity and depicting his efforts to ignore the world or reduce it to a pattern that suits his vision. When Pangall complains of the disturbance of his routine, the taunts and threats of the workmen, Jocelin waves him away with a reproach for his lack of faith, ignoring this member of his flock in the excitement of his apparently realized dream; ignoring, too, the fact of Pangall's impotence, which might call into question Jocelin's motives in arranging the marriage between the caretaker and Goody, his "daughter in God." Indeed, Jocelin's habit is to see people as less than human, as mere instruments of his vision. Again, his allegorical bent is suggested, especially in his recurrent descriptions of Gilbert, the young mute stonecutter engaged in carving busts of Jocelin to ornament the spire, and of Father Adam, his little chaplain. Gilbert's dumbness and Adam's obedience make them dear to Jocelin, for he feels they cannot oppose his will, and in his prideful blindness to their humanity he sees Gilbert as "doglike" and Adam as "the clothes-peg man" (pp. 19, 42).

As he at once manipulates and ignores Gilbert and Adam, so Jocelin attempts to deal with other people and situations. He alienates his friend and sacrist, Anselm, who opposes the building project, by taking over the man's duties as spiritual overseer of the workmen, and finds it easy to "erase" Anselm's friendship in the name of his vision; he likewise closes his eyes to the neglect of his duties caused by his involvement as overseer. He also increases the secularity of the project—hence of the church—by accepting dubious "gifts," such as the timber "given" by a nobleman in exchange for the bestowal of a canonry on his son, and the money "given" by his own aunt, Alison, venal former mistress of the previous king, in the hope of an honored burial place in the cathedral. Even Jocelin's spinal affliction, first manifested in a sensation of warmth at his back, is subsumed in his mysticism and his pride:

> It is my guardian angel.
> I do Thy work; and Thou hast sent Thy messenger to comfort me.
> As it was of old, in the desert.   (p. 18)

But Jocelin is not Christ, and his angel is also a devil who will take him up to a high place. And since both devil and angel exist within his own being, he cannot avoid acceptance of "the kingdoms of the world and the glory of them" (Matt. 4:8)—he is merely human, and for him there is no greater glory than the world as it is.

Perhaps Jocelin's most formidable human opponent is Roger Mason, the master builder, a man of strong will who constantly reminds the mystic of his vision's substance and paradoxical frailty—"'We've nothing but a skin of glass and stone stretched between four stone rods, one at each corner'" (p. 112)—and of the apparent inability of the foundations to sustain the spire's awesome weight. Jocelin finally sidesteps these objections and insures Roger's loyalty—while attempting to further submerge his own desires—by knowingly allowing the master builder to become entrapped in the "tent" of an adulterous relationship with Goody Pangall.

But his decision to condone the adultery of Roger and Goody is a fatal index of Jocelin's tendency to oversimplify complex human relationships and to underestimate the power of emotions, including his own. Inevitably, he finds the elements of his earthbound life rising around him like "a tide of muck" (p. 53), and he begins to realize that his spire is becoming inextricably involved with the fleshly life, that he is using "Roger and Rachel Mason, Pangall and his Goody—like four pillars at the crossways of the building" (p. 57). His angel alternately becomes a devil, torturing his spine as his illness increases and filling his dreams with sexual fantasy. At last his growing confusion and revulsion for the world of the flesh reach a climax in the phantasmagoric scene that closes chapter four, when the foundations of the spire begin to move "like the stirring of grubs ... like porridge coming to the boil in a pot" (p. 74). The charnel pit that Mason has dug to persuade Jocelin to abandon construction, already contaminated and odoriferous with seepage from long-forgotten graves, now suggests to Jocelin "the roof of hell" or "the living pagan earth, unbound at last and waking" (p. 75), giving conclusive notice of the connection between the high spiritual aspiration of his vision and its roots in the fleshly world of sin and death. And as if to bear out the earth's message, Mason's workmen—who are actually devil-worshipers—erupt in a ritual frenzy reminiscent of *Lord of the Flies* and *The Inheritors*, a frenzy that culminates in the murder of Pangall, whom they then bury in the pit as if to appease its gaping maw. Jocelin, shouldered aside by the crowd, sheltered by the broad form of Gilbert, and racked by his illness, fails to see Pangall's death. Even when he shortly afterward finds a sprig of ritual mistletoe above the pit, he recoils from its actual implications, transforming them instead into abstraction: "He found himself thinking of the ship that was built of timber so unseasoned, a twig in her hold put out one green leaf. He had an instant vision of the spire warping and branching and sprouting" (p. 90). But here, however abstractly, Jocelin's vision begins to grow.

The accelerating revelatory process of the next four chapters begins in a paradox familiar in Golding's fiction: the gaining of insight through physical isolation. Like Christopher Martin, Jocelin seeks isolation to avoid further insight, climbing the tower to remove himself from "all this confusion" below (p. 99). But his intial delight in the freedom of the heights is like that of "a small boy . . . when first he climbs too high in a forbidden tree" (p. 96). And Jocelin's spire is indeed to be his Tree of Knowledge, like the actual tree of Lok and Fa—or that of the young Golding himself. For from such heights as Jocelin scales, the temptation to look down is all but unavoidable. And looking down brings him back to the world that he wishes to escape, reminds him that he carries it inescapably within him. He finds the rounded landscape "soft and warm and smooth as a young body," and revolted by his "essential wickedness" turns his eyes upward (p. 101). At this point one notes the paradoxical tendency of the mystic to at once warp and transcend the truth, as Jocelin, thinking of St. John, sees a large bird and proclaims it to be an eagle. Gilbert, a "real artist" whose works have "no implication" or "temptation," sees the bird with unclouded eyes and shakes his head negatively (p. 102). In contrasting these two creators, a contrast not wholly unfavorable to Jocelin, Golding once more indicates the ambivalence of his own vision, the often uneasy poise between form and substance that he is attempting to equilibrate in *The Spire*.[5]

Gilbert's negative response turns Jocelin's eyes once more toward the earth, where he immediately receives a vision that demonstrates the value of combining the abstract and the concrete, and reminds the reader that Jocelin's vision, despite his self-deception, is indeed such a combination. As he watches the "procession of travellers" approaching the city, drawn by the growing spire, he sees

> In a flash of vision . . . how the tower was laying a hand on the whole landscape, altering it, dominating it, enforcing a pattern that reached wherever the tower could be seen, by sheer force of its being there. . . . The countryside was shrugging itself obediently into a new shape. Presently, with this great finger sticking up, the City would lie like the hub at the centre of a predestined wheel. New Street, New Inn, New Wharf, New Bridge; and now new roads to bring in new people.   (pp. 102–3)

This leads him to reflect on the widening of his vision: "I thought it would be simple. I thought the spire would complete a stone bible, be the apocalypse in stone. I never guessed in my folly that there would be a new lesson at every level, and a new power" (p. 103).

In the overall structure of *The Spire*, this glimpse of the larger world points up the novel's recognition, new to Golding's fiction, of a coherent social fabric, of the rhythms of social change, seen initially in the larger, more diverse cast of characters, in the clerical hierarchy, in the secularization of the church by the workmen, and by the outside "gifts." Indeed, Jocelin's story is seen to be part of a larger sociocultural process, the awakening of forces that led England from the Middle Ages into the Renaissance. And Jocelin's spire is central to this process, too, for the growing humanism of the Renaissance is nowhere more dramatically embodied than in its architecture, which at once allowed light and air into the cloistered atmosphere of the Romanesque medieval church and contributed to its secularization and—as some would have it—eventual corruption. The spiritual aspiration of the soaring Gothic cathedrals could not be expressed through faith alone; it demanded the work of skilled, often pagan, artisans, and exacted its cost—like Jocelin's spire—in gold and human lives. And the ornamentation of these cathedrals—like Gilbert's busts of Jocelin—records their history, encrusting the symbolic structures with "the life of 700 years ago, the life of the tavern and street, the sweaty, brawling, cruelly good-humored life that later congregated on the Left Bank or in Greenwich Village."[6] One may quibble, as some critics have done, with Golding's recreation of specific details of late medieval life; but ultimately such quibbles must yield to the fact that the novel, despite the intensity of its central drama, undeniably captures the flavor of the period and its sense of sociocultural turmoil.[7]

Jocelin forces himself to return to earth, reasoning that "no man can live his life with eagles" (p. 104). His heart, though, remains aloft, and his increasingly frequent ascents of the spire are a keynote of the swift sequence of revelations and plot developments that characterize the following three chapters. In chapter six, as Jocelin climbs toward "the strange peace of the tower" (p. 119), he overhears Roger and Goody making love in the master builder's makeshift planning-room, or "swallow's nest," bringing to him a shocking realization of how far his "daughter in God" has fallen, and how great has become "the cost of building material" (p. 121). In chapter eight that cost is driven home more deeply by his discovery of Goody's pregnancy, and by a climactic scene in which Rachel discovers and ends the adulterous relationship. Jocelin, approaching the caretaker's cottage with money to provide for Goody's period of confinement in a nearby convent, sees Rachel chasing Roger from the cottage and finds Goody crouched inside before the fire. The force of Rachel's assault and the shock of Jocelin's sudden appearance cause Goody to miscarry. But while her resultant death brings Jocelin horror and guilt, he still refuses to accept the sexual implications of his and Goody's relationship, though his mind fixes ironically on the refrain of an early English hymn, "Tomorrow Must Be My Dancing Day": *This have I done for my true love* (p. 132).[8]

Meanwhile, construction of the spire continues in halting and terrifying steps. Roger, prodded to brilliant innovation by Jocelin's obsessive demands, devises a steel band to strengthen the tower on which the spire's pinnacle will rest. And even after Goody's death, tortured by grief and guilt and Rachel's scorn, torn by his fear of heights and the tension of his task, Roger manages to contrive an ingenious means of strengthening the pinnacle against the wind (pp. 139–40). But at last the tension takes its toll, and when the pillars that support the tower are found to be bending, Roger breaks, leaving his duties to Jehan, his second-in-command. At this point Jocelin begins to spend more and more time with the men, actually sharing in their labors. But on the morning of Midsummer Day, the men refuse to work. And that night, alone on the spire, Jocelin sees fires on the distant downs, and realizes with a shock that his men must be among the devil-worshipers. Then, remembering the blood of Goody's miscarriage, the sprig of mistletoe, and the pit "dug at the crossways like a grave made ready for some notable" (p. 151, also p. 9), he pierces through the confused impressions to his submerged knowledge of Pangall's murder. And he descends to the crossways, where the replaced paving stones are "hot to his feet with all the fires of hell" (p. 151). This scene, which closes chapter eight, is perhaps Jocelin's most painful descent into his inner pit of guilt.

Chapter nine brings with it a partial abatement of confusion, a breathing space in which the reader may withdraw from the intensity of Jocelin's tragedy to a more detached and objective position. This development coincides with the arrival of the Papal Visitor, who comes with a Holy Nail for the spire and with authority to investigate the charges lodged against Jocelin by Anselm and other members of the order. Jocelin's interrogation by the Visitor again emphasizes the novel's broader context. Coming from Rome, acquainted with the world, the Visitor is shrewd and experienced enough to dismiss complaints, like those of Anselm, which arise from pettiness or envy; and he is wise and charitable enough to admire Jocelin's zeal. His humanism is a further indication of the larger changes in the ecclesiastical world that form the background of *The Spire*, and offers a worthy viewpoint from which to render judgment upon Jocelin. However, the Visitor halts in midinvestigation to allow the ravaged Jocelin to rest for a day, and the procedure is ultimately obviated by the events that swiftly follow.

That night, during a raging thunderstorm that threatens to topple the spire, Jocelin ascends the heights for the last time. Amid the confusion of darkness and lightning, the noise and physical onslaught of wind and rain and thunder, he drives the Holy Nail into the topmost point of the spire. And having completed this physical act, laden with sexual implication, he descends to a vision in which he at last identifies his innocent Goody with the red-haired devil of his dreams, after which he experiences "a wave of ineffable good sweetness, wave after wave, and an atonement" (p. 171).

But Jocelin's discoveries do not end with his discovery of the sexual dimension of his vision. A confrontation follows with Alison, during which he learns that even his rise in the church—which he had supposed to be an indication of his chosen status—is rooted in fleshly sin, a mere whim of the former king bestowed in recognition of the pleasure afforded him by Alison. Even the pillars of the cathedral, which Jocelin has regarded as symbolizing the faith of the original builders, are revealed to be a sham, filled with rubble in the age-old tradition of the corrupt builder. This revelation, which in one sense seems a mocking commentary on Jocelin's misplaced faith, may be seen, too, as a favorable contrast between the undeniable courage and aspiration of his vision—whatever its unconscious motivations and destructive results—and the small-minded corruption of the founding fathers. In any case, this moment is the occasion for Jocelin's final sacrifice to the spire, as he declares inwardly, "throw away, offer, destroy utterly, build me in with the rest of them" (p. 181).

And simultaneously with his declaration, Jocelin's illness strikes with full force: "Then his angel put away the two wings from the cloven hoof and struck him from arse to the head with a white-hot flail. It filled his spine with sick fire and he shrieked because he could not bear it yet he knew he would have to" (p. 181). The connection that Jocelin has attempted to deny between the spirit and the flesh, the mind and the body, the head and the arse, is here made strikingly explicit, and merges with the spire, which pierces to the clouds yet is founded on a foul pit. But Jocelin merely thinks in his agony, "I have given it my back" (p. 182), and begins to replace the spiritual aspect of his vision with his painful consciousness of the pit. As yet for Jocelin, life is a case of either-or.

Now he tries to reject his allegorical bent, tries to see man, not according to his wishes, but as he is. Regarding Father Adam from his deathbed, Jocelin sees "at once how mistaken they were who thought of him as faceless" (p. 189). But when Father Adam, after reading from Jocelin's notebook, describes the vision recorded there as representing a low level of prayer, the dying man still retains enough conviction to cry, "'My spire pierced every stage, from the bottom to the top!'" (p. 190). And though he is immediately struck by his "dark angel," as if in rebuke for his pride, Jocelin ultimately comes to realize that his spire, in a nontheological sense, does indeed "pierce every level." First, however, like Sammy Mountjoy, Jocelin must seek forgiveness. And like Sammy, he learns that forgiveness cannot be found. Anselm, like Rowena Pringle, cannot be reached by reason of his own self-deceit and inhumanity. And Roger, when Jocelin leaves his bed to seek him out, while at first embracing him in drunken recognition of their mutually fallen condition, cannot understand Jocelin's guilt-ridden mutterings, mistakes them in his own guilt as a call for retribution. Back in his room Jocelin hears of Roger's attempted suicide and thinks: "If I could go back, I would take God as lying between people and to be found there" (p. 212).

But Jocelin cannot go back. His only real comfort during this period, and the source of his ultimate understanding, is the at first inexplicable vision of an apple tree and a kingfisher that he experiences as he makes his way to Roger:

> There was a cloud of angels flashing in the sunlight, they were pink and gold and white; and they were uttering this sweet scent for joy of the light and the air. They brought with them a scatter of clear leaves, and among the leaves a long, black springing thing. His head swam with the angels, and suddenly he understood there was more to the apple tree than one branch. It was there beyond the wall, bursting up with cloud and scatter, laying hold of the earth and the air, a fountain, a marvel, an apple tree; and this made him weep in a childish way so that he could not tell whether he was glad or sorry. Then, where the yard of the deanery came to the river and trees lay over the sliding water, he saw all the blue of the sky condensed to a winged sapphire, that flashed once.   (pp. 196–97)

His first reaction is to reject what he has seen as another attempt at mystical vision—source of all the suffering he has caused: "I make too much fuss among the apple trees and the kingfishers" (p. 197). But the beauty of the bird and the tree is real, and remains in the back of his mind.

As he nears death, his attempt to curb his mystical tendencies swings him to the opposite extreme. He reduces his vision of the spire to its most physical level, seeing it as merely the result of his suppressed sexuality: "That's all, he thought, that's the explanation if I had time" (p. 213). He now regards Father Adam—the former "clothes-peg man"—from a new but still limited perspective, as "an extraordinary creature . . . covered in parchment from head to foot, parchment stretched or tucked in, with curious hairs on top and a mad structure of bones to keep it apart" (p. 214). And finally, rejecting the religion that has caused his former self-deception, he thinks of his fellow men: "*How proud their hope of hell is. There is no innocent work. God knows where God may be*" (p. 214).

But Jocelin's attempt to deny the spiritual world is no more successful than his efforts to ignore the physical. Like Sammy Mountjoy, he is finally exposed to the Sphinx's riddle. Unlike Sammy, though, Jocelin finds an answer—perhaps, significantly, because the riddle is embodied for him in a physical entity, not merely a series of words. Moments from his death, Jocelin's unfocused vision sees what seem to be two "eyes" peering at him.

Then, abruptly, the two "eyes" slide together, and are revealed to be the window, "bright and open." And there, outlined against the sky, is his spire,

> still and silent, but rushing upward to some point at the sky's end, and with a silent cry. It was slim as a girl, translucent. It had grown from some seed of rose-coloured substance that glittered like a waterfall, an upward waterfall. The substance was one thing, which broke all the way to infinity in cascades of exultation that nothing could trammel.   (p. 215)

The world of the spirit is resurrected. And overcome by the contradiction of the two worlds, Jocelin thinks in panic, "'Now—I know nothing at all'" (p. 215). But, in a sudden flash "like a bluebird over water," the two worlds in Jocelin's mind slide together like the unfocused window and become one. He realizes that he and his vision are indeed, like the bird's flight, transitory; but that his spire is a thing of enduring substance, comprehending guilt and innocence, joy and terror, creation and destruction. Remembering the sweetness of the angelic leaves and blossoms in the garden, remembering that the tree's pure physical beauty is also an age-old emblem of the Fall, Jocelin finally sees how good and evil, beauty and ugliness, can be one, how formal significance and physical substance may embrace such a paradox. And with his dying breath, he strives to cry out, "'*It's like the apple tree!*'" (p. 215).

Here, in this dramatic recognition scene, Jocelin's story attains tragic significance in a way that Sammy Mountjoy's never does. This is not to say that every novel need be tragic, but it is an index of the degree to which Golding realizes in *The Spire* what he merely seems to be striving for in *Free Fall*. Jocelin confronts the confusion of the world and accepts it as Sammy never does; he also resolves the paradox of form and substance, by recognizing that in substance is contained all form, and that to see any form one must first perceive substance. In a sense, Jocelin's experience—and perhaps Golding's—is that of an allegorist who discovers symbolic vision. Jocelin's spire suggests a multiplicity of meanings: it is at once a diagram of prayer, a stone ship, a phallus, a hammer, a human spine from head to arse, an apple tree. But before all these it is a physical structure. Perhaps in this fact is the simplest key to understanding the novel and to evaluating Golding's accomplishment. For *The Spire*, in its acceptance of the artist's primary responsibility to the substance of his creation, indicates Golding's recognition of something that he had perhaps in the past known only unconsciously. His known tendency to balk at the multiplicity of meanings that critics had seen in his earlier works is the clearest indication of that possibility.[9] *The Spire* constitutes Golding's—as well as Jocelin's—admission of the symbolic, rather than merely allegorical, suggestiveness of his work, his recognition of the truths that are expressed willy-nilly by a devoted and skillful artist in the act of molding substance into form.

This discovery on Golding's part, like all of his artistic motivations, prompts him in *The Spire* to examine the source of his insight. Thus, as *Lord of the Flies* examines Ballantyne's *Coral Island*, and *The Inheritors* examines Wells's *Outline of History*, *The Spire* examines the construction of the Salisbury spire, a work not only of imagination, but of physical reality, involving real people and real historical action.[10] These facts account not merely for the novel's sense of the physical world—not unusual in Golding's fiction—but also for the greater depth and breadth of characterization, the greater degree of human drama and social consciousness. The characters are Golding's most vital, most human, exhibiting a range of motivation and behavior, a capacity for dynamic interaction, far beyond that seen in any previous novel. The social background not only adds to the sense of reality, but also complements the central symbolic drama with its suggestion that not merely Jocelin, but the medieval church, society itself, is involved in tasting of the knowledge of good and evil.

And of course, Jocelin's tragedy, with its intense contrast of the physical and the spiritual, represents an impressive achievement for Golding. Working with material that most modern authors—well acquainted with Freud—would recoil from for its apparent obviousness, Golding creates a complex structure of plot and characterization that acknowledges the fact of psychosexual motivation, and yet transcends it by relegating it to its proper place in the larger sphere of human reality. The novel does have flaws, in particular a tendency to obscurity that arises from the limited viewpoint, causing many readers, for example, to miss the fact and later ramifications of Pangall's murder. But such obscurities seem, as usual, a result of Golding's intransigent insistence that his readers face in the difficult riddles of his fiction a measure of the complexity that has become his theme. In any case, *The Spire* seems to mark the end of a phase in Golding's fiction, preparing the way for new confrontations of that complexity, and for new methods of exploring its labyrinthine ways.

7.

The Pyramid:
Innovation, Rediscovery, Challenge

In the final chapter of their study of Golding, Mark Kinkead-Weekes and Ian Gregor sum up his first five novels as follows: "the twelve years' work can be seen as an exploration of the problem of disengaging myth from fable, and of giving it a sufficiently historical location." They conclude that in *The Spire* Golding finds such a historical location for his symbolic vision, and that the novel resolves the "predominant tensions" of his work, "leaving the artist free for further exploration." Though *The Spire* does approach more closely than its predecessors the particularity and substance of the mode that Kinkead-Weekes and Gregor call "history" and which John Peter calls "fiction," its medieval setting and tragic intensity seem to set it somewhat apart from the main currents of the contemporary novel.[1] *The Pyramid* (1967) may be seen as resulting from Golding's "further exploration" of the fictional mode, and especially from his confrontation of the more purely social aspects of reality.

The novel comprises three overlapping but essentially independent sections, each set in the tiny English village of Stilbourne and narrated by the protagonist, Oliver, whose growth from childhood to middle age is the book's main connecting thread. The independence of the parts is underscored by the fact that two of the three had appeared in periodicals as long short stories, the first in *Kenyon Review* as "On the Escarpment," the third in *Esquire* as "Inside A Pyramid."[2] The first part of the novel finds Oliver on the verge of entrance into Oxford in the early 1930s, torn between his love for music and the prospect of a career in chemistry, between his chaste and hopeless passion for the soon-to-be-married Imogen Grantley and his desire for the accessible body of Evie Babbacombe, the "local phenome-

non."[3] His seduction of Evie is accompanied by his first real consciousness of guilt, and the section ends with his realization of
the opportunity he has lost to "discover" her true humanity.
The second, previously unpublished segment covers Oliver's unwilling involvement in the petty quarrels and rivalries of the Stilbourne Operatic Society at the end of his first Oxford term, and
his encounter with Evelyn De Tracy, the grotesque and probably
homosexual professional director hired to produce the Society's
version of *The King of Hearts*. At the conclusion of this episode,
during a comically disastrous performance of the sentimental
operetta, Oliver loses another opportunity for human discovery
through his immature and insensitive response to a drunken but
well-meant gesture of self-revelation by De Tracy. *The Pyramid*
is completed by the middle-aged Oliver's return to Stilbourne in
1963, a visit that triggers a chain of reminiscences dating back
to his childhood, of his relationship with his former music
teacher Miss Dawlish, better known as "Bounce," and of her
role in determining his future. This section, wider ranging than
the first two and less centrally concerned with Oliver, also treats
Bounce's relationship with Henry Williams, a mechanic who
turns the lonely spinster's love for him to his own advantage,
though in a process too ambiguous to invite simple moral judgment. The novel does conclude with another demonstration of
Oliver's lack of humane insight. This time, however, he is ultimately granted recognition of his failing; and the self-knowledge
brings with it not only a sense of guilt and resignation, but also
an awakening of his human sympathies that softens somewhat
the book's otherwise bleak conclusion.

  The Pyramid is informed throughout by the prevailing note of
irony that is so apparent in all of Golding's work; but the narrative tone, perhaps best described as tragicomic, is new—at
least in the degree to which it is employed here. Golding once
characterized *Pincher Martin* as "a blow on behalf of the ordinary universe," and perhaps his subsequent novels may also be
identified as such.[4] However, as one may conclude from the direction of his development through *Free Fall* and *The Spire*,
Golding has come to believe that such blows may best be struck
by attempting to recreate that universe in terms more comprehensive, less symbolically intense. Denis Donoghue, in a review
of *The Pyramid*, goes even farther, proposing that Golding

would perhaps "like nothing better than to write a loose baggy monster of a novel, possessed of life to the degree of irrelevance." Donoghue's judgment is that as an attempt, even on a more modest scale, to write such a novel, *The Pyramid* is "an embarrassment, a disaster," because Golding's imagination is "alien to memory."[5]

In dealing with a writer of Golding's stature, one feels compelled to reexamine his apparent failures—like *Free Fall*—to avoid judgments based on misunderstanding of their purposes, and to measure their possible contributions to the further development of his art. *The Pyramid* does seem to represent an effort by Golding to explore the life of social man through fuller commitment to the mode of fiction, or as Donoghue would have it, memory. And memory is indeed an appropriate term in relation to *The Pyramid*. Oliver's story is an exercise in reminiscence; and more importantly, the novel is full of correspondences to Golding's life and earlier works. In *The Pyramid*, as in his previous novels, Golding reexamines the sources of the insight that motivates the work at hand; this time those sources are traceable in large part to his own past. Knowing Golding's methods, one may be less than surprised that his first real "autobiographical" novel was written only after it could be sufficiently justified by thematic and technical necessity.

Oliver and his family live in a cottage much like the boyhood home in Marlborough that Golding describes in "The Ladder and the Tree" (*The Hot Gates*, pp. 166–75); and Marlborough is clearly the counterpart of Oliver's Stilbourne, sharing with it a number of geographical features, including its proximity to Barchester, the fictionalized Salisbury of *The Spire*. Oliver's uneasy poise between the attractions of music and chemistry parallels that of the young Golding between science and literature; and his entry into Oxford to pursue a scientific career is mainly influenced, as was Golding's similar course of action, by the gentle and diffident rationalism of his father. Indeed, one may trace to "The Ladder and the Tree," and to another autobiographical essay called "Billy the Kid" (*The Hot Gates*, pp. 159–65), numerous details in *The Pyramid*: Oliver's father's fascination with the wireless and the gramophone (compare *The Pyramid*, p. 156, and *The Hot Gates*, pp. 168–70); the scholastic crisis that leads to Oliver's commitment to science (*The Pyra-*

mid, pp. 165–66; *The Hot Gates*, pp. 172–75); the character of Oliver's mother (*The Hot Gates*, pp. 159–60, 163); the pervasive sense of social hierarchy that paralyzes life in Stilbourne (*The Hot Gates*, pp. 167–68). Even Goldings's frustrated poetic ambitions are allusively incorporated in *The Pyramid* when Oliver retreats in confusion from an attempt to read a modern poem. Reflecting on his earlier consignment of music to the status of a hobby, he observes: "I was a scientist with one private vice. I was expecting too much if I thought myself clever enough for two" (p. 93). In fact, Oliver, who goes on to become a successful scientist, may well be Golding's projection of what he might have become had he not switched from scientific to literary studies after his second year at Oxford.

Oliver, unlike Golding, follows a typical line of development, both in his choice of career and his ultimate regard—albeit touched with a sense of frustration and loss—for the arts as diversions, hobbies, not to be confused with the seriousness of everyday life and work. One need only compare Oliver with such atypical protagonists as Christopher Martin, Sammy Mountjoy, and Dean Jocelin to recognize the high degree of Golding's commitment in *The Pyramid* to examining the "ordinary universe." Striking, too, in comparing the novel with its three immediate predecessors, are its echoes of various features of the earlier works, some merely incidental, others more substantial, but all contributing in some way to the creation of *The Pyramid*'s ordinary world.

The structure of *The Pyramid* invites comparison with *Pincher Martin* and *Free Fall*, since all three novels incorporate discontinuous time schemes and flashbacks. Golding's purposes differ, of course, from one novel to the other: the flashbacks in *Pincher Martin* are hardly intended as a coherent, substantial study of Martin's life and times; and *Free Fall*, too, is ultimately more concerned with Sammy than his surroundings. But the fact remains that both novels were assailed for their failure to create a sufficiently convincing sense of social reality, a sense that is definitely present in *The Pyramid*. The time scheme of *The Pyramid* is much less puzzling, less liable to misunderstanding than those of the earlier books: unburdened like Chris by the fear of reality, or like Sammy by the desire for significance, Oliver narrates clearly and at a leisurely pace; the self-completeness of each episode leaves the reader free to draw parallels and infer thematic relationships at will, without obvious authorial manipulations. Indeed, *The Pyramid* seems much like a second version of *Free Fall*, with more substantially realized—because more autobiographical—plot and characters and less overt concern with the problems of significance and communication that were apparently resolved in *The Spire*.

Oliver's seduction of Evie is a more complex process than Sammy's attempt to possess Beatrice, since Oliver's is a real social world, inhabited by mothers, fathers, rivals, gossiping neighbors, uninterested bystanders, full of the complications and distractions of everyday life and work in a small town. The preliminary sparring between Oliver and Evie, and the actual seduction scene itself, involve the most explicit sexual descriptions (pp. 55–56, 62) that Golding had written prior to *Darkness Visible*, realizing graphically an image that had appeared more tentatively in both *Free Fall* and *The Spire*. In *Free Fall* the child Sammy's innocent drawing of rolling hills and woodlands is distorted by the sexually frustrated Rowena Pringle into a libidinous fantasy (pp. 205–6); and in *The Spire* Jocelin's similar frustration produces a like response to the wooded landscape that he sees from the tower (p. 101). *The Pyramid* transforms these internal projections into external reality, as for Oliver the clump of trees on the escarpment that overlooks Stilbourne is the "hot and sexy" haven where he wishes to have Evie.

The erotic passages in *The Pyramid* are notably different from those of *Free Fall* in their exploration of the complexity of both characters involved. Indeed, though Oliver is as concerned with exploitation as was Sammy, he is overwhelmed by Evie's womanhood like "a small boat in a deep sea" (p. 62), and is himself personally humiliated when she uses him as an object of revenge against Stilbourne, forcing him to make love to her on the bare escarpment in full view of the town, and particularly of Oliver's father, who sees the couple through his binoculars.

The final meeting between Oliver and Evie, two years later, after his entry into Oxford and her establishment as a woman of the world in London, leads to a violent quarrel and the inadvertent self-revelation by Evie of an earlier incestuous relationship with her brutal father. In the midst of his anger Oliver suddenly realizes that Evie has acquired for him "the attributes of a person rather than a thing," that he and she might have "made something, music, perhaps, to take the place of the necessary, the inevitable battle." But Evie leaves to disappear forever from Oliver's life, and he returns home "confounded, to brood on this undiscovered person and her curious slip of the tongue" (pp. 90–91).

The "making of music" mentioned by Oliver becomes, as the novel progresses, more than a romantic cliché. The inscription on the cross that Evie wears—*Amor vincit omnia*—merges with an oft-quoted pronouncement of Miss Dawlish's father—"Heaven is music"—and the combination of music and love takes on a symbolic significance, opposing the exaltation of science represented mainly by Oliver's father.

The central part of *The Pyramid*, involving Oliver with Evelyn De Tracy and the Stilbourne Operatic Society, takes up thematically where the first leaves off, dramatizing the Stilbourne syndrome, the inability of the townspeople to "make music together." *The King of Hearts* is a disharmonious fiasco that De Tracy is powerless to rescue; his theatrical knowledge is irrelevant here, since the real problem lies in the snobbery, small-mindedness, and essential selfishness of the assembled representatives of English society. Though much of the episode aims at being humorous, the underlying theme is clearly serious, a fact emphasized by the conclusion, in which the homosexual De Tracy responds to Oliver's youthful desire to know "the *truth* of things" (p. 123) by showing the young man a photograph that pictures the director in a ballerina's costume. Oliver's laughter drowns out all hope of communication, and masked in the grotesquerie of the scene is the fact that the two are playing in a different key: Oliver wants to know the truth of things like a scientist; De Tracy proffers a greater truth—about people—emphasizing the need for perception. Oliver's perception at this point, however—a year away from his last meeting with Evie—is unequal to an understanding of De Tracy. And though the producer does awaken him to the stupidity, vanity, and insensitivity of his romantic ideal, Imogen Grantley, the section ends not with a real increase in Oliver's perceptiveness, but with his smug confidence of his superiority to the disharmonious throng.

The third part of *The Pyramid* emphasizes both the music-love-science symbolism and the novel's relationship to *Free Fall*, fusing the two elements and integrating them skillfully into the central symbol of the pyramid. The child Oliver, shuttling back and forth across the street between his father's rationalism and Miss Dawlish's music lessons, parallels the child Sammy, torn between the gentle scientism of Nick Shales and the fierce religiosity of Rowena Pringle. The paired adult characters are certainly similar: Nick is a science teacher and Oliver's father a chemist; both Rowena and Bounce are love-starved spinsters teaching spiritually oriented subjects. In one scene, after he has seen Oliver and Evie on the escarpment, Oliver's father echoes closely Nick's vehement sentiments on sex: "—this man what d'you me call him—these books—cinema—papers—this sex— it's *wrong, wrong, wrong!*" (p. 81; compare with *Free Fall*, p. 231). But Oliver's father is a more complex character than Nick, more human and less clearly functional; from an autobiographical standpoint one may see Nick as an idealization of Golding's father, and Oliver's father as a more realistic portrait. Bounce Dawlish, too, is far deeper and more various than Rowena Pringle; a mannish, pipe-smoking old maid whose own ambivalent love for music has been sternly inculcated in her by an eccentric father, Bounce is in fact *The Pyramid*'s most interesting character.

Bounce's musical relationship with Oliver (whom she nicknames "Kummer" in a rare joking mood) is intertwined with her frustrated love for Henry Williams, an intinerant young Welsh mechanic who persuades her to buy the town's first car, and after endearing himself to her eventually settles in Stilbourne as a general handyman, mysteriously producing a wife and child in the fashion of many an old ballad. The Williamses finally move into Bounce's house as lodgers, and for years Oliver's music lessons afford him glimpses of the strange ménage, of Bounce's frustrated and pathetic attempts to capture Henry's attention, of Henry's use of Bounce's money to establish himself as a prosperous garage owner. But Oliver betrays the same insensitivity to the unattractive Bounce that he had shown in his encounter with De Tracy, though again he may be partially excused by his youth, the influence of the Stilbourne environment, and his parents' persistent and irritating assertions of his devotion to his music teacher.

Bounce's thwarted love for Henry diminishes her capacity for love of music. And in turn she plays her part in turning Oliver from music to science, unexpectedly seconding his father's advice while prophetically equating him with Henry: "'Don't be a musician, Kummer, my son. Go into the garage business if you want to make money. As for me, I shall have to slave at music till I drop down dead'" (p. 163). On his last visit to Stilbourne, while seated at her grave, Oliver concludes that his assumed devotion to Bounce has actually been hatred, stemming from his childhood fear of her Gothically gloomy house and her own forbidding exterior; from his oppression at her role in turning him from music and at the grotesque relationship between her and Henry's family. Oliver laughs at the irony of the inscription that Henry has had cut on her tombstone: her father's unctuous epigram, Heaven is Music. But shortly afterward, while visiting her empty house, he comes upon the smashed, burnt ruins of Bounce's music, and he is jolted by the realization that Bounce has destroyed it out of despair, out of her inability to find solace in the harmonies so inhumanely taught by her father or the selfish love that Henry rationed to her like dividends from the capital she had invested in his business. The pyramid of the title becomes symbolically one with the defeated possibilities of music and love in the ruins of Bounce's pyramid-shaped, crystal-encased metronome (pp. 150, 182). And Oliver realizes that he, like Henry, has evolved into a selfish rationer of love, incapable of reaching out to another human being, of paying the "unreasonable price" of himself as Bounce did on the day when her mind snapped, when in her last all-out attempt to win Henry's attention she paraded naked down the streets of Stilbourne (pp. 174–75).

The theme of human blindness to the necessity for selfless love is explicitly identified in The Pyramid's epigraph, taken from the Instructions of Ptah-Hotep, the primal Egyptian deity, creator of gods and men and, significantly, the patron of art and science and builder of the first pyramid: If thou be among people make for thyself love, the beginning and end of the heart. Both the epigraph and a further dimension of Golding's symbolic use of the pyramid are present in germinal form in Free Fall: in Sammy's aphorism, "Love selflessly and you cannot come to harm" (p. 33), and in a remark upon his adolescent sensitivity to "the shape of our social pyramid" (p. 193). And the overall symbolic aspect of *The Pyramid*'s theme is foreshadowed in Sammy's fascination with the kings of Egypt.

Perhaps the most useful source of insight into Golding's symbolism in *The Pyramid* is "Egypt from My Inside" (*The Hot Gates*, pp. 71–82), in which he discusses his lifelong interest in Egyptology.[6] Here, he identifies modern man with the ancient Egyptians in the capacity for banality, greed, and cruelty, and speaks of "our ant-like persistence in building a pyramid of information" (p. 81), drawing a parallel between modern man's exaltation of science and the purely scientific aspect of the Egyptian pyramids. But despite these similarities, and despite the social tyranny and "ponderous self-advertisement" (p. 73) represented by the ancient pyramids, Golding nonetheless accepts them as the stuff of vision, "the thumbprint of a mystery" (p. 81). For it is the secret within the pyramid that makes it, like Jocelin's spire, a true symbol, "that which has an indescribable effect and meaning" (p. 74). In the depths of the tomb is the puzzling answer to the Sphinx's riddle of *Free Fall*: "Man himself . . . timelessly frozen and intimidating, an eternal question mark" (p. 74).

Turning to *The Pyramid*, one sees clearly how it embodies the ideas that Golding discusses in "Egypt from My Inside." The novel treats the social aspect of the pyramid—its banality and hierarchical preoccupation, its exaltation of science over art—from base to apex. But it focuses, too, on the mystery, the human enigma that Oliver, bound by artificial social strictures and his growing faith in science, ignores until almost too late. With De Tracy, Oliver misses the mystery almost entirely; with Evie, he senses it incompletely, and merely in relation to her. Only with Bounce Dawlish, appropriately enough after a visit to her grave, while seated amid the relics of her life, does Oliver get inside the pyramid to confront the "eternal question mark" that is man. Only from this confrontation does he gain a measure of insight into his own humanity and that of others, the knowledge that in looking at Henry Williams he sees his own face, that of a man who will "never pay more than a reasonable price" (p. 185). But though Oliver drives away from Stilbourne as a man who cannot "love selflessly," he is at least aware of his condition. And the bleak consolation of self-awareness is the most that Golding's novels offer to the majority of men as a possible source of qualified salvation.

Clearly, *The Pyramid* is much more complex than most of its early reviewers and critics have found it to be. The book is as symbolically dense as any of Golding's previous novels while at the same time dealing more extensively with the contemporary world and exploring new dimensions of characterization and human interrelationship. Much of the added social breadth and detail of the novel stems from its autobiographical aspects; much remains in Oliver's story, however, that cannot be easily traced to autobiographical sources, or to the working out of its intricate symbolic pattern. A close reexamination of the book reveals that here again, as in *Free Fall*, Golding's imagination apparently challenges the vision of a towering literary figure: *The Pyramid*, Golding's first real attempt at a social novel, seems to parallel ironically *Great Expectations*, by England's greatest social novelist, Charles Dickens. Oliver's story corresponds, in a number of important respects, to that of Pip, the protagonist of Dickens's book.[7]

The parallel is suggested even by general likenesses: both novels deal with the central theme of spiritual blindness, as caused both by the pressures of society and individual obsession; both emphasize in similar ways the power of selfless love and count the cost in guilt and wasted lives of blindness to its necessity; both are first-person narratives of a young man's journey in such darkness to a somber self-awareness of his guilt in middle age; both possess an anecdotal flavor and a tendency to derive both humor and insight from human eccentricity and the ironic possibilities of an immature narrator. The books even have a similar history of publication, appearing first in parts and later as completed works, a common practice in the eighteenth and nineteenth centuries, but notably less so today.

More specific correspondences are numerous. *The Pyramid* opens, like *Great Expectations*, with the protagonist's coerced involvement in a clandestine errand of mercy to a nearby marsh: Oliver is persuaded by Evie to help push Bounce's car, in which Evie and his neighbor Bob Ewan have been joyriding, out of a pond. Oliver's home life is much like Pip's, since his mother is as dominant as, if less offensive than, Mrs. Joe. Like Pip, Oliver, infatuated with a shallow, vain girl of higher station—Imogen Grantley—fails to see the worth of an accessible girl of lower station—Evie—and loses both. In a scene highly reminiscent of the low-born Pip's questionable triumph over Herbert Pocket for the attentions of Estella, Oliver employs roughhouse tactics to best Bob Ewan, his social superior, in a fight for Evie's favors. Much of Oliver's inner life is dominated, like Pip's, by a rejected spinster who lives in a house of Gothic proportions and atmosphere, a house he returns to in later life to acknowledge his hatred of the woman, only to find her earthly remains—in Bounce's case, her music—ravaged by fire, softening his attitude and causing him to "forgive" her. On Oliver's return from London to his hometown he also confronts Henry Williams, whose tradesman's homespun manner and ultimate success seem to indicate his correspondence to Joe Gargery, and whose profession—garage mechanic—is the twentieth-century equivalent of Joe's. Indeed, Henry is the one person who suspects, but keeps, the secret of Oliver's involvement in the affair of Bounce's car, paralleling Joe's silent knowledge of Pip's thefts on behalf of Magwitch. Occupying a central place in both novels, though Golding treats it at greater length, is the protagonist's encounter with a grotesque actor, an encounter that crystallizes the theme of each novel: Wopsle's self-deceiving "great expectations" are merely a more ludicrous version of Pip's, and the entire episode, like Oliver's experience with De Tracy, demonstrates the young man's lack of perception and human sympathy. There are other parallels, even extending to such minor details as Oliver's name (recalling one of Dickens's best-known child heroes), and his being dosed, like Pip, with "opening medicine" at the slightest sign of emotional instability.

The intent of such a relationship would seem twofold: to render Golding's criticism of the modern world more trenchant; and more importantly, to revise Dickens's novel, both thematically and technically. On the one hand, Golding underscores by comparison with Dickens's fictional world the banality and meanness of his own; in almost every instance described above, the modern characters are distinctly diminished in moral or dramatic stature by comparison with their nineteenth-century counterparts, and their world, consequently, is a duller, less hopeful place. But this is precisely Golding's point. For the world of *The Pyramid*, unlike that of *Great Expectations*, is carefully pruned of any sentimentality that might soften its somber theme. Conversely, however, the issue of guilt is deliberately clouded in *The Pyramid* to emphasize the complexities that plague modern man's attempts either to affix or accept moral responsibility.

For if Golding's characters suffer by comparison with those of Dickens, they are in a sense more realistic: Bounce Dawlish, for all her grotesqueness, is much less bizarre than Miss Havisham, and Bounce's role in determining her young pupil's future is far smaller, his hatred of her far less justified; and Henry Williams, unlike Joe Gargery, is hardly selfless and simple, though these are traits that he attempts to project. Indeed, in the sort of switch that Golding is so fond of, Henry Williams is a more plausible villain of *The Pyramid* than is Bounce. One can imagine Golding's reasoning here: "Who is more likely to hold sway over people's lives in modern society, an eccentric old lady or an entrepreneur?" Even here, however, the issue is complicated, for Henry's sin is, like Oliver's, merely his inability to "pay more than a reasonable price" in his dealings with his fellows.

And just as there are no clearcut villains in *The Pyramid*, there is an absence of Dickensian melodrama and coincidence, digression and repetition. Golding's novel is trimmed of Orlicks and Magwitches: they contradict the real universe. And *The Pyramid* avoids entirely the city of London, which provides much of the sprawling populousness of *Great Expectations*, concentrating instead on Stilbourne, which like Pip's boyhood home is the ultimate repository of revelation, guilt, and atonement.

But though *The Pyramid* succeeds in presenting a more realistic and concentrated embodiment of its themes than does *Great Expectations*, it does so at considerable cost in other important fictional elements. Golding's apparent reduction of Dickens's world to a size that corresponds to the world of his own vision demonstrates not only the persistent single-mindedness of that vision, and his confidence in his own powers, but also his evident limitations as a writer. For if *The Pyramid* creates a world more typical than that of *Great Expectations*, and presents an accurate picture of modern man's isolation from his fellows, it also sacrifices Dickens's wider sense of humanity, his love of eccentric, larger-than-life types, and his delight in weaving a complex and fascinating web, not primarily of symbols, but of human action. And perhaps more important, *The Pyramid* sacrifices the high dramatic tension, not only of Dickens's novel, but of Golding's own earlier works.

The Pyramid shows Golding once more in a state of artistic flux, expanding his own vision beyond its former limitations, but at the same time unwilling to abandon himself completely to chaos. Unlike Dickens, he is not yet, and perhaps will never be, a writer who "revels in the vitality of the ordinary universe." *The Pyramid* is incisive in its portrayal of Stilbourne and its people; and the subtlety of its symbolic patterns stands as an impressive technical achievement. Donoghue clearly overstates when he says that Golding "writes of ordinary things with extraordinary awkwardness."[8] But the fact does remain that, compared with the human riches of Dickens, Golding's characters and their relationships seem somewhat tritely conceived and his novel more akin to such narrow chronicles of small town banality and eccentricity as *Main Street* and *Winesburg, Ohio* than to *Great Expectations*. Then, too, Golding's attempts at humor in *The Pyramid* compare badly with Dickens: the irony that Golding uses so well as an element of tragedy seems heavy-handed when he applies it to the creation of comic effects, a fault also notable in his play, *The Brass Butterfly*; his attempts at more boisterous comedy—as when he describes in sexual imagery Oliver's frantic attempts during *The King of Hearts* to get onstage through a narrow passageway with his beefeater's halberd—are often so flatfooted as to be embarrassing.[9] Despite its faults, however, *The Pyramid* does represent a definite extension of Golding's range, and perhaps may best be regarded, like *Free Fall*, as a necessary stage in his developing fictional confrontation of the contemporary world.

Perhaps the major difficulties that Golding faced in working out his expanded vision may best be seen by focusing on two related features of his first six novels. The first of these features was his tendency, as in *The Pyramid*, to use works by other writers as ironic foils of his own, his tendency to say, like Sammy Mountjoy, "Not that—but this!" (*Free Fall*, p. 102). John Bowen sees in Golding's assertive individualism a kind of arrogance, "as if all his fellows walking their more usual technical paths but lighting them with their own personal lights were doing something he scorned to do."[10] Golding's novels sometimes do give this impression; and a further indication of such an attitude was Golding's initially steadfast refusal to recognize readings of his novels based on such studies of human nature as the works of Freud and Frazer.[11] Of course, a writer must stand or fall not by what he reacts to or by what he intends, but by what he creates, and Golding's creative record is impressive. But one must conclude that in *The Pyramid* Golding's reactive tendencies—whether arrogant or not—betray him somewhat: the parallel of *Great Expectations* causes him to fall between two stools, since the obviously reductive process involved acts in opposition to his equally obvious attempts to extend his fictional range.

The second feature of Golding's works that needed resolution if his new approach to fiction were to succeed was his apparent inability to find in the contemporary social world more than the vitiated drama and tragedy of such characters as Oliver and Sammy Mountjoy. Of his first six novels, only *The Spire*, which is far from contemporary, seems to offer a fully integrated blend of the historical and the tragic. Perhaps, though, the answer lay not, as Martin Green had it, in Golding's "sullen distate for the contemporary," but in his choice of protagonists.[12] Golding's art, reactive as it is, seems to require as a protagonist a foil of sufficient stature to allow his vision the detachment it needs to realize its full dramatic power. In his latest three novels through 1967, only one protagonist, Jocelin, was a successful foil; Sammy and Oliver—perhaps because of their autobiographical aspects—seem too close to Golding to lend themselves to such treatment. This requirement of a foil, so much akin to his use of literary parallels, is at once Golding's most striking limitation and a major source of his unique power.

The Pyramid seemed to represent, for most critics, another crucial stage in Golding's career, one that would demand of him continued widening of his vision, continued exploration of the technical resources of his craft, perhaps even an attempt to break free from the reactive pattern that had held him throughout his writing life. The ordinary universe, as Donoghue observed, might prove to be "beyond [Golding], or beneath him."[13]

The Pyramid

Perhaps, however, Golding's new declaration of oneness with the ancient Egyptians—with their "unreason, spiritual pragmatism, and capacity for ambiguous belief" (*The Hot Gates*, p. 82)—gave promise of a new commitment to the everyday world.

8.

Darkness Visible:
Infinity and Triviality

The years immediately following publication of *The Pyramid* gave scant indication of a "new Golding." The appearance in 1971 of *The Scorpion God* seemed little more than a holding action. Comprising three novellas, *The Scorpion God* does reflect several of Golding's characteristic interests: the classical period, in the previously published "Envoy Extraordinary" (1956); prehistory, in "Clonk Clonk," which deals, like *The Inheritors*—though far less seriously—with the adventures of a group of early men; and Egyptology, in the title piece, which centers on the death of a pharoah from the late Middle Kingdom and the efforts of his jester—the Liar—to avoid perishing according to custom with the ruler. Perhaps the most notable development in this collection is Golding's sympathetic (if ironic) treatment of two antiheroic protagonists: the Liar in "The Scorpion God" and Chimp in "Clonk Clonk." As Virginia Tiger observes, *The Scorpion God* is "minor Golding," though she notes in its prose a tonal modulation, perhaps an earnest of Golding's new willingness to treat the human dilemma "movingly, gently, even genially."

Tiger also notes in her 1974 study Golding's stated intention to write a novel "about England."[1] Not until 1979, however, with the publication of *Darkness Visible*, did the long-awaited major work appear. The novel takes its title from Milton's description of Satan's surroundings immediately after the Fall:

A dungeon horrible, on all sides round
As one great Furnace flam'd, yet from those
    flames
No light, but rather darkness visible.[2]

98

And the epigraph—*Sit mihi fas audita loqui*—comes from Aeneas's prayer to the gods in Book Six of *The Aeneid*, where the hero asks that he be allowed to speak of the Underworld:

> allow me to retell what I was told;
> allow me by your power to disclose
> things buried in the dark and deep
>   of earth![3]

These solemn allusions seem to promise a return to Golding's earlier tendency to view man's fallen nature through the filter of the past, rather than a novel about contemporary England.

But *Darkness Visible* is a rare creation: here Golding achieves for the first time a successful fusion of the historical and the contemporary. More importantly, this novel, set largely in England and spanning almost four decades from World War II through the late seventies, displays a new breadth of focus for Golding. Not only is the book virtually panoramic in its portrayal of English society, it also marks an innovative departure from Golding's characteristic approach to viewpoint. Though he retains the final qualifying shift of perspective that Tiger terms "ideographic," Golding does not here confine himself in the balance of the novel to the perceptions of one major character; rather, he creates what for him is a virtual cacophony of voices. Part of the book does take the form of a first-person journal kept by one of the characters; but the major portion is presented through the eyes and voice of a wryly ironic, omniscient narrator who effaces himself frequently to focus on the viewpoints of four major characters and numerous minor ones. And these several interior voices are themselves augmented by dialogue, which Golding uses more tellingly and extensively than ever before: some fifty characters assume "speaking roles" in this drama, their number and social range again far exceeding the scope of any other Golding novel.

The major incident of the story can be recounted simply. An exclusive boys' school in the typically English town of Greenfield becomes the target of a terrorist kidnapping attempt. The kidnappers are led by twin sisters, Sophy and Toni, Greenfield natives and daughters of a local celebrity, chess expert Robert Stanhope. The plot, doomed from the beginning by the authorities' foreknowledge, is further thwarted by the heroism of a disfigured handyman, Matty Windrove. Innocently involved on the periphery of the crisis are three other characters: Sim Goodchild, a bookseller and neighbor of Stanhope; Edwin Bell, a schoolmaster at Greenfield's other school, Foundlings, for orphaned boys; and Sebastian Pedigree, a town nuisance and ex-schoolmaster at Foundlings, discharged years earlier in a scandal stemming from his homosexuality. Golding's concern in *Darkness Visible* is to explore the circumstances and motivations that bring about the convergence of these diverse characters in an event that seems increasingly symbolic of contemporary experience. In that exploration Golding creates a more convincing portrayal than ever before of the bonds between fate, free will, and accident, and of the ways in which human life partakes of both infinity and triviality.

By treating the lives of his main characters—Matty and Sophy—from childhood, Golding invests the novel's outcome with a sense of destiny fulfilled. At the same time, he is at pains to provide ironic leavening to that portentous structural scheme. Matty Windrove is another in the line of Golding's saintly mystics who, like Simon, Nathaniel, and Lok, seem to be natural victims. Unlike those predecessors, however, Matty's self-sacrifice is willing, successful, and not without humor, and his character is portrayed much more thoroughly. Sophy, too, is a familiar type in Golding's novels, one of the guilty—like Jack Merridew, Tuami, Pincher Martin, Sammy Mountjoy, and Jocelin—whose obsessive self-will brings torture to themselves and others. Like Matty, Sophy is a more thorough portrait than most of her earlier counterparts, with the possible exception of Sammy Mountjoy; and because Sophy is a less autobiographical character than Sammy, presented from a less subjective viewpoint, she stands as Golding's most successful foil in a contemporary setting.

The novel begins with that quintessential watershed in contemporary English experience: London during the Blitz. Yet seen through the eyes of a fireman whose peacetime occupation is bookseller, the fire from a German air raid transforms a corner of London through its "shameful, unhuman light" into "a version of the infernal city."⁴ And out of that apocalyptic inferno walks the naked and nameless infant, horribly burned, who is to be one of the novel's four major characters and the pivot of all subsequent action. This opening scene is strikingly effective, combining matter-of-fact naturalistic dialogue and description with richly allusive imagery to suggest the supernatural aura surrounding the child's inexplicable emergence from the flames.

The child, whose origins are never uncovered by the authorities, is initially identified as "number Seven" prior to his progress through a series of hospitals. He is finally named at the insistence of a matron, but even that arbitrarily imposed label—Matthew Septimus Windrove—is confused through a clerk's whimsy and her chief's indecision. Thereafter, throughout the novel, Matty's surname is garbled by other characters, a perpetual emblem of his vague origins.

"Born from the sheer agony of a burning city" (p. 20), Matty is transferred to Foundlings School in the town of Greenfield, the novel's major setting. More pathetic than any of Dickens's orphans by reason of his disfigurement, Matty is misunderstood, baited by his classmates, and ultimately turned out of the school. But, as in *The Pyramid*, Golding's Dickensian allusions here are ironic: Foundlings, "maintained by two of the biggest trade unions in Britain," (p. 21), is no Dotheboys Hall, nor even a Salem House. Matty is victimized not by monsters like Squeers or Creakle, but by all-too-human figures: his well-meaning but expedient headmaster, and Sebastian Pedigree, a repressed homosexual master whose obsession with attractive young boys and revulsion at Matty's appearance precipitate the novel's second major crisis. Admonished by the headmaster about rumors concerning him, Pedigree cancels tutorial sessions with his current favorite and, as a penance, begins working instead with Matty. Henderson, the rejected favorite, commits suicide, leading to Pedigree's dismissal and imprisonment, for which he irrationally blames the innocent Matty. As a result of Matty's confused response to interrogation about the catastrophe, the headmaster removes him from the school as ineducable. The boy finds himself set to work running errands in another Dickensian relic: Frankley's, an ironmonger's that retains the character of the Industrial Revolution even while grudgingly accepting the "enormities" of plastic.

Despite its gloomy architecture and outmoded practices, Frankley's is no more actively antagonistic toward Matty than the school that had benignly deprived him of an education.

Of Earth and Darkness

Amid this "complex disorder of ancient and modern, this image in little of society at large" (p. 42), Matty's appearance assures that he will merely be ignored. But the tension generated as he becomes more aware of both his effect on others and his sexuality turns him increasingly inward. Hopelessly attracted to a shopgirl at Frankley's, he wanders distractedly one Sunday amid Greenfield's few landmarks, pausing notably at Sim Goodchild's bookshop and at the parish church. At each place he experiences a revelation of sorts, the first perhaps genuinely mystical, the second ironically, even comically, so (pp. 47–50). In any case, these events send Matty on an obsessively introspective search for his identity and purpose in life. Spurred by his misconceived but lingering sense of guilt concerning Mr. Pedigree and by his defensive flight from "the daughters of men," the innocent Matty's pilgrimage leads him as far as Australia before bringing him back, years later, to the destiny for which, like one of Hardy's protagonists, he seems to have been created.

Matty's experiences in Australia turn him away more and more from human contact and deepen his commitment to religious mysticism. Wearing a broadbrimmed hat and long hair to hide his external scars, Matty finds inner solace in the matter-of-fact rituals of the Old Testament and in the mysteries of the New, particularly the Book of Revelation. But Golding portrays Matty's naive faith with considerable irony.

In a scene that perfectly illustrates Golding's narrative method in *Darkness Visible*, Matty becomes lost in what he imagines to be the Outback, actually the suburbs of Darwin, and wandering in thirsty delirium, he encounters a naked aborigine. Matty takes the abo to be what he appears: an ignorant primitive. Instead, the abo is a wily local character named Harry Bummer, a hater of whites who has "'never been the same since they made that film about him'" (p. 65). Matty, attempting to communicate with Harry through a combination of sign language and rudimentary English, sketches a cross that the abo associates with both the white man's religion and the British airplanes that mean the advent of nuclear testing in Australia. In a grotesquely comic sequence, Harry equates the two—"'Fucking big sky-fella him b'long Jesus Christ'" (p. 64)—and not only subjects Matty to a humiliating mock crucifixion, but also jumps on his groin. Believing himself permanently neutered, Matty takes the experience as a further clarification of his own isolation from ordinary humanity.

After a brief period of increasingly eccentric behavior interpreted by Australian officials as antinuclear protestation, Matty sets sail once more for England. And having given the reader a compassionate, ironically humorous, circumstantial account of Matty's development into a man apart, Golding thereafter adopts for him the limited viewpoint familiar from previous novels, using the device of a journal in which Matty vividly and touchingly depicts his own self-abandonment to the mystical—or hallucinatory—direction of two ghostly presences like prophesying angels out of Revelation. And these spirits guide Matty back to Greenfield, directing him to accept a position as handyman at Wandicott House School, where he labors for over ten years in relative content, having been assured that he is "near the centre of things" (p. 95) and that his destiny involves a child (p. 101). Shortly after his return, while on an errand in the town, Matty sees two little girls, "beautiful like angels," entering Goodchild's bookshop (p. 101). Warned by his spirits to avoid the town and such temptations, he resolves to "trust that there are good spirits (angels) looking after the little girls which of course there are" (p. 102).

This tenuous crossing of paths is the nearest approach to contact between Matty and the Stanhope twins until the novel's climactic scenes. In the ten years between, however, the angelic-looking little girls become quite different creatures. Paired by birth and in the eyes of outsiders, the twins are alike neither physically nor mentally: Toni, pale-haired and ethereal, is inclined to lose herself in things around her; Sophy, dark and conventionally beautiful, is passionately self-absorbed. As children, the two are forced by the adult world to be "everything to each other" (p. 118): their mother flees from her failed marriage to faraway New Zealand; their austere, distant father becomes increasingly preoccupied with his chess and with the series of resident "aunties" who cater to his physical needs. The twins, banished to living quarters in the stables, become in adolescence more and more hostile to the adults around them and more and more competitive with each other. Toni characteristically escapes from self by directing her alienation outward in systematic action; Sophy, driven by an inchoate incestuous attraction for her father, turns more completely inward to what she calls "weirdness," the attempt to control others through force of will. But when the twins finally drive away the last of the "aunties"— a jovial, devious Australian named Winnie—Sophy cannot be sure whether to credit her own "weirdness" or Toni's more practical exposure of Winnie's infidelity to Mr. Stanhope. And when in their late teens Toni emulates her mother's flight from England, eventually to join a group of international terrorists, Sophy refuses to follow suit, confirmed in her sense that she belongs to no one but herself, the creature "sitting inside with its own wishes and rules at the mouth of the tunnel" (p. 123), and still more determined in her desire "to bring the impossibilities of the darkness . . . into being to disrupt the placid normalities of the daylight world" (p. 134).

Through that emblem of contemporary Western civilization, the transistor radio, Sophy learns that her "weirdness" is ESP; she also hears of entropy, and finds the concept "obvious" (p. 131). The polar opposite of Matty, with his belief in universal order and divine guidance, Sophy is convinced, like Pincher Martin and his "centre," that what exists beyond all else is the assertion of self. And in *Darkness Visible*, Sophy is Golding's major vehicle for his most direct exploration to date of contemporary England and its mores. In his previous novels, Golding had treated sex briefly and obliquely or, at most, with considerable restraint; here, in language of unprecedented bluntness, he focuses directly and in some detail on a variety of sexual relationships, including homosexuality.[5]

Sophy chooses her own moment of sexual initiation, allowing herself to be picked up in Greenfield by a passing motorist. She finds the act itself "trivial," and considers a subsequent brief experiment with prostitution "boring"; but she notes the potential of sex as an instrument of her will and half-recognizes it as a physical locus of the undirected hate within her (pp. 135–39).

After Toni's departure, Sophy, too, leaves Greenfield for London, where a time-filling job at a travel agency and a mundane social life increase her ennui and frustration. She allows herself to drift into a relationship with a "ponderously respectable" civil servant, Roland Garrett, who takes her at face value, assuming that they will eventually marry. But during a visit to Greenfield, Sophy's bored acquiescence to Roland's clumsy love-making erupts into rage, and she plunges a tiny ornamental knife into his shoulder. For the first time she experiences orgasm:

> Something strange was happening. The feeling from the blade was expanding inside her was filling her, filling the whole room. The feeling became a shudder then an unstoppable arching of her body. She cried out through her clenched teeth. Unsuspected nerves and muscles took charge and swept her forward in contraction after contraction toward some pit of destroying consummation into which she plunged.
> Then for a timeless time there was no Sophy. No *This*. Nothing but release, existing, impossibly by itself.   (p. 146)

And the experience, merging with her childhood memory of a similar moment when she had killed a duckling (pp. 108–9), gives her a new sense of identity.

Almost immediately thereafter, Sophy leaves her job and falls in with Gerry, a young ex-army officer turned petty criminal with whom she discoveres a kinship both physical and spiritual. Nonetheless, she finds that taking part in small-time robberies with Gerry and his friend Bill—a former enlisted man—hardly answers her need to make her inner darkness visible to the daylight world. And when she learns that another former army colleague of Gerry's, Fido Masterman, is a physical training master at Wandicott House—now catering to the scions of oil-rich Arabs—she conceives a kidnapping plot. Putting the plot into motion gives Sophy ample opportunity to impose her will: first, in mobilizing the reluctant Gerry and Bill; second, in gaining access to Wandicott House through the clownish and muscle-bound Fido, to whom she becomes "engaged." It is during this period that Sophy encounters Matty Windrove directly for the first and only time when she returns to the school for a final reconnaissance in the guise of a search for her "lost" engagement ring. Pretending at last to find the ring, she attempts to strengthen her story by giving credit to the inarticulate odd-job man with the "awful face," unaware that Matty has witnessed her deception.

At this crucial juncture, beset by her own doubts concerning the logistics of the scheme and disgusted by Gerry's squeamishness, Sophy retreats to her childhood home. And in one of the novel's many powerful scenes, Sophy's incestuous desire for her father pushes its way to the surface: "before him, her unbra'd breasts . . . hardened, stood out and lifted the fabric of her shirt as clear as if it had been shouted" (p. 186). But she finds herself unable to act. Furious at this failure of nerve, she strengthens her resolve that there will be "other occasions for outrage" (p. 188). Significantly, however, it is only the return to England of Toni and her associates that allows Sophy the means to translate the kidnapping from idea into action. And it is Sophy's inability to act, stemming from her incapacity for self-abandonment, that ultimately diminishes her.

Meantime, the ingenuous Matty, confused rather than suspicious, interprets the incident of the engagement ring as a divine portent that, ironically, triggers for him a last triumphal vision on the thirteenth anniversary of his first. In this revelation three spirits appear, the newcomer clad "all in white and with the circle of the sun around his head," and Matty is informed that the unknown boy he is charged with guarding "shall bring the spiritual language into the world and nation shall speak it unto nation" (p. 239). Matty records this vision in his journal, confident that his young charge will someday read it. But Matty interrupts this entry, his last, to leave for a meeting with Edwin Bell, for whom Matty has become a kind of guru, and the more skeptical Sim Goodchild, who is all but paralyzed by middle-aged disillusionment and self-doubt. Matty hopes that this meeting will also provide him an opportunity to make his peace with Mr. Pedigree, now a town embarrassment who still blames Matty, rather than his own pederastic obsession, for his social and professional downfall.

But the meeting never takes place. Delayed by a flat tire on his bicycle, Matty is knocked unconscious by one of the terrorists, who have begun a diversionary assault as planned by Sophy. Almost immediately a bomb explodes, igniting a petrol tank and engulfing Matty—for the second time in his life—in flames. This scene is the occasion for one of Golding's most compelling descriptive passages. As Bill runs past the fire with the boy, wrapped in a blanket, in his arms,

> . . . a strange thing happened in the fire. It seemed to organize itself into a shape of flame that rushed out of the garage doors and whirled round and round. It made as if on purpose for the man and his burden. It whirled round still and the only noise from it was that of burning. It came so close to the man and it was so monstrous he

dropped the bundle and a boy leapt out of it and ran away, ran screaming to where the others were being marshalled. The man dressed as a soldier struck out wildly at the fire-monster, then ran, ran shouting away into the cover of the trees. The fire-monster jigged and whirled. After a time it fell down; and after some more time it lay still.   (p. 248)

Sophy, waiting in safety near the town, sees the light from the fire hanging above the downs, "her own fire, a thing she had done, a proclamation, a deed in the eye of the world—an outrage, a triumph!" (p. 250). And her elation becomes a surge of desire for the ultimate assertion of self. In a scene reminiscent of Jack Merridew's encounters with pigs in *Lord of the Flies* (pp. 27, 125), Sophy is seized by a vision of what she will do to the captive boy:

She thrust with all the power there was, deliriously; and the leaping thing inside seized the knife so that the haft beat in her hand, and there was a black sun. There was liquid everywhere and strong convulsions and she pulled the knife away to give them free play but they stopped. The boy just sat there in his bonds, the white patch of elastoplast divided down the middle by the dark liquid from his nose.
(p. 252)

But then Bill arrives to report not only the failure of the kidnapping, but also that Gerry has joined Toni in flight with the hapless Fido as their hostage. In a paroxysm of frustration and jealousy, she rages that her sister is: "'Just ideas. Ghosts. Ideas and emptiness, the perfect terrorist'" (p. 253). Sophy's defeat is more profoundly underscored, however, by her concern—again like Pincher Martin—for mere self-preservation, reducing her ultimately to a shaming caricature of helpless femininity:

"I shall tell. I was used. They'll have nothing on me. . . . I've been very foolish my lord I'm sorry I can't help crying. I think my fiancée must have been part of it my lord he was friendly with, with—I'm sure my daddy had nothing to do with it, my lord. He wanted us out of the stables my lord, said he wanted to use them for something else. No my lord that was after he had been to a chess meeting in Russia. No my lord he never said."   (pp. 253–54).

Powerful as the novel's climax may be, Golding characteristically provides the reader with a complicating shift of perspective. In a final chapter, he writes from the viewpoint of the ordinary man in the persons of Sim Goodchild and Edwin Bell;

107

then he enters the mind of the outcast Mr. Pedigree. Both Good-child and Bell are smarting under public ridicule, principally be-cause of two related events: first, a meeting between Sim, Edwin, and Matty that had taken place with Mr. Stanhope's permission some days before the kidnapping in the twins' vacant rooms, during which the three had conducted a session of wordless spir-itual communion; second, a brief encounter with the disguised Toni when Sim and Edwin had arrived at the Stanhope stables for another meeting with Matty on the night of the kidnapping. Public revelation of these meetings, recorded through govern-ment television surveillance and later used as evidence, proves acutely embarrassing to the two old friends. Edwin, zealous would-be disciple of Matty, vows in outrage to "'write a book about the whole affair'" and "'find out the truth'" (p. 258). The skeptical Goodchild, however, recognizes his own mundaneness, a blend of "infinity and triviality" (p. 200) that cannot break down the partitions between people, insuring that "one is one and all alone and ever more shall be so" (p. 225). For Sim, "'No one will *ever* know what happened. There's too much of it, too many people, a sprawling series of events that break apart under their own weight'" (p. 258). Nonetheless, when the two men hear a news report about Matty's journal, which the police hope will "throw some light," both are heartened, as if it may briefly penetrate the partitions that keep the human self in "solitary confinement" (p. 261).

Christlike in his self-sacrifice, Matty may also be seen as a latter-day version of his biblical namesake, heralding the advent of a new messiah. Does his journal throw the light of prophecy upon the events of the novel, or is it a record of coincidence that obscures those events in "darkness visible"? The answer de-pends on one's willingness to take a self-abandoning leap of faith. Golding does seem to suggest that the partitions can be broken—if only momentarily—by some such escape from self, subjective transformed into objective, thought into action. Seen from this viewpoint, Matty and Toni are the only characters in the novel who obey the divine injunction in Revelation 3:15: "I would thou wert cold or hot." All of the others—and none more than Sophy—are paralyzed by self. Far from endorsing commit-ment to belief in such exegetic systems as theology and politics, however, Golding's novel takes its central theme from the journal entry in which Matty observes: "What good is not breathed into the world by the holy spirit must come down by and through the nature of men" (p. 238).

The primacy of this theme, echoing the epigraph from *The Pyramid*—"If thou be among people make for thyself love, the beginning and the end of the heart"—is emphasized in the final scene of *Darkness Visible*. Mr. Pedigree, returning to the public park he has haunted in hopeless pursuit of boys, fearful that his obsession may one day make him a murderer, suffers a fatal heart attack. And in his agony he recognizes that the dead Matty alone had loved him all along. Then Matty, in Pedigree's dying vision, undergoes a third immolation, one that transforms him into a god who, like Pincher Martin's, shows compassion beyond human understanding by separating the old man from his obsession through death. And in a final ironic comment on human understanding, a parkkeeper sees Mr. Pedigree from a distance and supposes him to be asleep: "He knew the filthy old thing would never be cured and he was more than twenty yards away when he began talking at him bitterly" (p. 265).

Darkness Visible is quite obviously the most circumstantially complex novel that Golding has written. He captures and exploits contemporary idiom and society more thoroughly than ever before, especially in dealing with sexuality, and does so through an unprecedentedly huge array of memorable characters. Yet Golding does not abandon his previous themes and forms: he merely expands upon them. He does not abandon the ideographic method; he increases its complexity, continuing his movement beyond the duality that dominated his earliest work. He does not abandon the rich allusiveness of his previous novels. He does, however, move beyond his past tendency to take a reactive or revisionist approach to the work of earlier artists. In fact, if *Darkness Visible* represents a reaction of any sort, it is to Golding's own vision and techniques, for it is full of echoes, modifications, and elaborations of elements from his other novels. Above all, *Darkness Visible* is a highly successful example of the novelist's art, a sprawl of events and characters, that emphatically does not "break apart under its own weight," rendered in arresting language that does, indeed, "throw light" on what it means to be human.

A new Golding novel, *Rites of Passage*, is scheduled for publication in 1980; and based upon the evidence of *Darkness Visible*, one would anticipate continued technical exploration and further definition of his increasingly complex vision. But whatever Golding does in the future, his past accomplishments place him among the most striking and significant writers of his generation, author of works at once difficult and exciting, characterized by a vision of brilliant insight and intransigent integrity. Golding the artist, like Sammy Mountjoy, has always been and will continue to be—in the midst of success or failure—"a creature of discovery" (*Free Fall*, p. 102).

Notes

Introduction

1. Lionel Trilling, "Lord of the Flies," *The Midcentury*, p. 10.
2. Golding made this remark in a letter to me, 17 May 1966.

1: Indices and Influences

1. This lecture, originally presented at UCLA, appears under the title of "Fable" in William Golding, *The Hot Gates*, pp. 85–101. Further parenthetical references in the text are taken from this edition. For more of Golding's own commentary on his life and work, see Jack I. Biles, *Talk: Conversations with William Golding*.

2. Golding, "The Ladder and the Tree," *The Hot Gates*, p. 168.

3. James R. Baker, *William Golding, A Critical Study*, p. xiv.

4. Bernard S. Oldsey and Stanley Weintraub, *The Art of William Golding*, pp. 7–8.

5. E. L. Epstein, "Notes on William Golding and Pincher Martin," afterword to Capricorn Edition of *Lord of the Flies*, p. 249. Included in the Putnam's Casebook Edition of *Lord of the Flies*, edited by James R. Baker and Arthur P. Ziegler, Jr.

6. Baker, *A Critical Study*, p. xvii.

7. Baker, *A Critical Study*, pp. 7–10, 14–15. The classical influence may also be seen in Golding's novella, "Envoy Extraordinary," which first appeared in a collection called *Sometime Never: Three Tales of Imagination*, pp. 11–78. This witty tale of an urbane Roman emperor's successful attempt to sidestep the problems attendant on scientific and technological progress also appears in Golding's novellas collected under the title of *The Scorpion God*; Golding also adapted the piece, retitled *The Brass Butterfly*, into a sort of neo-Shavian stage comedy as a vehicle for the distinguished British actor, Alastair Sim.

8. Oldsey and Weintraub, *The Art of William Golding*, p. 8

9. See Baker, *A Critical Study*, p. xv. See also *Talk*, pp. 30–33.

10. John Peter, "The Fables of William Golding," *Kenyon Review*, p. 583. This essay may also be found in part in Baker and Ziegler's Casebook Edition of *Lord of the Flies*, and in full, with a postscript, in William Nelson, *William Golding's Lord of the Flies, A Source Book*.

11. This "Introduction" from Ian Gregor and Mark Kinkead-Weekes's "School Edition" of *Lord of the Flies*, pp. i–xii, is quoted as it appears in Baker and Ziegler's Casebook Edition of the novel, pp. 236, 243.

12. Mark Kinkead-Weekes and Ian Gregor, *William Golding, A Critical Study*, p. 256.

13. Golding in an interview with Frank Kermode, "The Meaning of It All," *Books and Bookmen*, p. 9; also in part in Baker and Ziegler, Casebook Edition, pp. 197–201.

14. Virginia Tiger, *William Golding: The Dark Fields of Discovery*. Tiger emphasizes Golding's manipulation of viewpoint in a structural pattern involving a "first movement" and a "coda" that emphasizes Golding's view of human existence as typified by paradox.

2: *Lord of the Flies*

1. Golding as quoted in E. L. Epstein, "Notes on William Golding and Pincher Martin," Capricorn Edition of *Lord of the Flies*, p. 250. See also "The War as Awakening" in Jack I. Biles, *Talk: Conversations with William Golding*, pp. 30–52.

2. Golding, *Lord of the Flies* (New York: Coward-McCann, 1955), pp. 30, 186; further parenthetical references in the text are taken from this edition.

3. Frank Kermode, "Coral Islands," *The Spectator*, p. 257; also in William Nelson, *William Golding's* Lord of the Flies: *A Source Book*, pp. 39–42. Carl Niemeyer, "The Coral Island Revisted," *College English*, pp. 241–45; also in Nelson, pp. 88–94, and Baker and Ziegler, Casebook Edition, pp. 217–23.

4. Frank Kermode and William Golding, "The Meaning of It All," *Books and Bookmen*, p. 10.

5. Lionel Trilling, "*Lord of the Flies*," *The Midcentury*, p. 10.

6. Howard Babb, in *The Novels of William Golding*, pp. 26–28, takes a contrary view of this passage, stressing its "visual richness" and "precise diction," and praising Golding's care in creating what Babb terms "the plausible experience of a terrified boy." I would agree with Babb's reading of all but the imaginary (or hallucinatory) dialogue.

7. See Golding's brusque reaction to such a sexual reading of the scene in James Keating, "Interview with William Golding," in Baker and Ziegler, Casebook Edition, p. 195; see also Bernard F. Dick, "The Novelist Is a Displaced Person: An Interview with William Golding," *College English*, pp. 480–82.

8. See James R. Baker, *William Golding: A Critical Study*, p. 8, for comparison with *The Bacchae*, and William Golding, *The Hot Gates*, pp. 161–62, for a possible autobiographical source.

9. See Donald R. Spangler, "Simon," in Baker and Ziegler, Casebook Edition, pp. 211–15.

10. See Louis J. Halle, "Small Savages," *Saturday Review*, p. 16, and James Gindin, *Postwar British Fiction*, pp. 196–206, both of which appear in Nelson, *A Source Book*, Halle, pp. 5–6, and Gindin, pp. 132–40.

11. Keating, "Interview with Golding," p. 194.

12. E. L. Epstein, "Notes on Golding," p. 250.

13. See Mark Kinkead-Weekes and Ian Gregor, *William Golding: A Critical Study*, p. 64. See also "Piggy" in *Talk*, pp. 11–14, where Golding points out that the description of Piggy as "true" and "wise" is not the author's, but Ralph's.

14. See Frederick R. Karl, *A Reader's Guide to the Contemporary English Novel*, p. 259.

Notes

15. Kinkead-Weekes and Gregor, *A Critical Study*, p. 19. See also Babb, *Novels of Golding*, pp. 7–34, for a similar defense of Golding's narrative power.

16. Frank Kermode, "The Novels of William Golding," *International Literary Annual*, p. 18; this article also appears in its entirety in Nelson, *A Source Book*, pp. 107–20, and in part in Baker and Ziegler, Casebook Edition, pp. 203–6.

3: *The Inheritors*

1. H. G. Wells, as quoted in *The Inheritors* (New York: Harcourt, Brace & World, 1962); further parenthetical references in the text are taken from this edition.

2. See Bernard S. Oldsey and Stanley Weintraub, *The Art of William Golding*, pp. 43–72; Oldsey and Weintraub also speculate in this chapter on *The Inheritors*'s connection with a novel of the same title by Joseph Conrad and Ford Madox Ford; see especially pp. 44, 54–55, 69.

3. See Kenneth Rexroth, "William Golding," *The Atlantic*, p. 96–98. Rexroth, in an unusually vituperative attack on Golding, sees his first three works merely as failed attempts to overturn Ballantyre, Wells, and Defoe.

4. See Mark Kinkead-Weekes and Ian Gregor, *William Golding: A Critical Study*, p. 117, for a discussion of Golding's alterations in the original manuscript of *The Inheritors*, showing how the novel "arrives at a vision richer than its apparent thesis."

5. James Gindin, *Postwar British Fiction*, p. 198.

6. As quoted in John Bowen, "Bending Over Backwards," *Times Literary Supplement*, p. 608; this essay also appears in William Nelson, *William Golding's* Lord of the Flies: A Source Book, pp. 55–60.

7. Bowen, "Bending Over Backwards," p. 608.

8. Kinkead-Weekes and Gregor, *A Critical Study*, p. 69. For further detailed discussion of viewpoint in *The Inheritors* see also Howard Babb, *The Novels of William Golding*, pp. 43–61, and Virginia Tiger, *William Golding: The Dark Fields of Discovery*, pp. 68–85.

9. William Faulkner, *As I Lay Dying*, p. 59.

10. See Sigmund Freud, *Totem and Taboo*, trans. James Strachey, pp. 135–36, 141–43.

11. See Sigmund Freud, *Civilization and Its Discontents*, trans, James Strachey, pp. 78–80.

12. Gindin, *Postwar British Fiction*, pp. 199–200. This essay originally appeared in *Modern Fiction Studies*, pp. 145–52.

4: *Pincher Martin*

1. See Frederick Karl, *A Reader's Guide to the Contemporary English Novel*, p. 259.

Of Earth and Darkness

2. Though Martin's island is ultimately revealed as his own desperate creation, its geographical analogue is Rockall, an actual island west of the Hebrides.
See Jack I. Biles, *Talk: Conversations with William Golding*, pp. 73–74.

3. See James Gindin, *Postwar British Fiction*, pp. 201–2, and Karl, *Reader's
Guide*, pp. 258–59.

4. William Golding, *The Two Deaths of Christopher Martin* (New York: Harcourt, Brace & World, 1957), p. 7; the title of this first American hardcover
edition of *Pincher Martin* reflects the early critical confusion concerning Martin's
death; further parenthetical references in the text are taken from this edition.

5. Jack I. Biles and Carl R. Kropf, "The Cleft Rock of Conversion: *Robinson
Crusoe* and *Pincher Martin*," in *A William Golding Miscellany*, pp. 27–28.

6. E. C. Bufkin, "*Pincher Martin*: William Golding's Morality Play," in *A William Golding Miscellany*, pp. 5–16.

7. See William Golding, *The Hot Gates*, pp. 166–67. See also Virginia Tiger,
William Golding: The Dark Fields of Discovery, pp. 120–27, for a thorough
discussion of the symbolic role of the cellar and darkness, a motif that Golding
takes up again in *Free Fall*.

8. Bufkin, "Morality Play," pp. 14–15.

9. Frank Kermode and William Golding, "The Meaning of It All," *Books and
Bookmen*, p. 10.

10. For a fuller discussion of the parallel to the biblical creation see Mark
Kinkead-Weekes and Ian Gregor, *William Golding: A Critical Study*, pp.
135–53.

11. Compare with Daniel Defoe, *Robinson Crusoe*, pp. 45–46, 57–61.

12. Bufkin, "Morality Play," p. 7.

13. Bernard S. Oldsey and Stanley Weintraub, *The Art of William Golding*,
pp. 75–78, 81–83, 95–96. See also Ian Blake, "'Pincher Martin,' William Golding, and 'Taffrail,'" *Notes and Queries*, pp. 309–10.

14. James R. Baker in his *William Golding, A Critical Study*, pp. 45–47,
shows in discussing this scene that Martin's dialogues with God need not be
taken literally as evidence of Golding's Christian orthodoxy.

15. See Tiger, *Dark Fields*, pp. 106–10, and Howard Babb, *The Novels of
William Golding*, pp. 88–92. Babb offers an interesting reading of the "coda"
(to use Tiger's term) that sees Davidson, the naval officer, as playing Death to the
crofter Campbell's Everyman. This view further underlines Martin as a mere
usurper of the Everyman role.

16. Peter Green, "The World of William Golding," *Transactions and Proceed-
ings of the Royal Society of Literature*, p. 50.

17. Kinkead-Weekes and Gregor, *William Golding, A Critical Study*, p. 156.

18. John Peter, "The Fables of William Golding," *Kenyon Review*, p. 591.

19. Remark in an unpublished interview by Owen Webster, as quoted in
Baker, *Golding*, p. 56.

20. John Peter, "Fables," p. 591.

Notes

5: *Free Fall*

1. William Golding, *Free Fall* (New York: Harcourt, Brace & World, 1960), p. 9; further parenthetical references in the text are taken from this edition.

2. Jack I. Biles, *Talk: Conversations with William Golding*, pp. 78–81.

3. Frank Kermode, "The Novels of William Golding," *International Literary Annual*, p. 27.

4. John Peter, "The Fables of William Golding," *Kenyon Review*, p. 577.

5. The prototype for Beatrice in Golding's fiction is obviously Mary Lovell of *Pincher Martin* (see pp. 147–49); for an earlier version of his coupling of beauty with inner vacuity, see "Pish and Tush," William Golding, *Poems*, p. 31.

6. See also Virginia Tiger, *William Golding: The Dark Fields of Discovery*, pp. 155–56, who suggests in this scene a further parallel to *La Vita Nuova*.

7. In his final confrontation with E. C., Stephen turns on the "spiritual-heroic refrigerating apparatus, invented and patented in all countries by Dante Alighieri." See James Joyce, *Portrait of the Artist as a Young Man*, p. 252.

8. Joyce, of course, uses the Daedalus myth, and Lawrence builds upon the myth of Pluto and Persephone—see George H. Ford, *Double Measure: A Study of the Novels and Stories of D. H. Lawrence*, pp. 28–47.

9. Mark Kinkead-Weekes and Ian Gregor, *William Golding, A Critical Study*, p. 194.

10. Virginia Tiger shares this view (see *Dark Fields*, pp. 144–47). And while Howard Babb (*The Novels of William Golding*, pp. 116–19) praises *Free Fall*'s "adventurous" style, he nonethless notes weaknesses in narrative form and characterization.

11. Ian Gregor and Mark Kinkead-Weekes, "The Strange Case of Mr. Golding and His Critics," *The Twentieth Century*, pp. 115–25. This essay offers a digest of adverse criticism of *Free Fall* from various sources.

12. Tiger, *Dark Fields*, p. 165.

6: *The Spire*

1. William Golding, "An Affection for Cathedrals," p. 35.

2. See Jack I. Biles, *Talk: Conversations with William Golding*, pp. 99–100. See also Virginia Tiger, *William Golding: The Dark Fields of Discovery*, p. 176.

3. James R. Baker, *William Golding, A Critical Study*, p. 75. Perhaps Jocelin's tragedy is more Sophoclean than Euripidean, since it bears much resemblance to *Oedipus Rex*.

4. William Golding, *The Spire* (New York: Harcourt, Brace & World, 1964), p. 3; further parenthetical references in the text are taken from this edition.

5. Golding, "Cathedrals," p. 42; compare *Free Fall*, p. 15.

6. Golding, "Cathedrals," p. 42.

7. For criticism of *The Spire*'s lack of authentic medieval detail, see especially Raymond Carter Sutherland, "Medieval Elements in *The Spire*," in *A William Golding Miscellany*, pp. 57–65.

8. Tiger, *Dark Fields*, pp. 177–78, points out echoes in *The Spire* of motifs from Golding's "Miss Pulkinhorn," also set in Salisbury Cathedral, which appeared in 1960 as both radio play and short story.

9. See James Keating, "Interview with William Golding," Casebook Edition of *Lord of the Flies*, pp. 192–93, and Frank Kermode, "The Meaning of It All," *Books and Bookmen*, p. 9.

10. In Bernard S. Oldsey and Stanley Weintraub, *The Art of William Golding*, pp. 125–45; Oldsey and Weintraub again indicate other possible parallels, from Eliot to Ibsen to Browning.

7: *The Pyramid*

1. Compare Mark Kinkead-Weekes and Ian Gregor, *William Golding, A Critical Study*, pp. 239–57, and John Peter, "The Fables of William Golding," *Kenyon Review*, p. 577.

2. William Golding, "On the Escarpment," pp. 311–400; and "Inside a Pyramid," *Esquire*, pp. 165–69.

3. William Golding, *The Pyramid* (New York: Harcourt, Brace & World, 1967), p. 7; further parenthetical references in the text are taken from this edition.

4. Frank Kermode and William Golding, "The Meaning of It All," *Books and Bookmen*, p. 10. See also Leighton Hodson, *William Golding*, pp. 101–9, for a discussion of Golding's use of the "tragicomic" mode.

5. Denis Donoghue, "The Ordinary Universe," pp. 21–22.

6. Significantly, this essay first appeared as "Egypt and I" in *Holiday*, several months before the publication of "Inside a Pyramid" (see note 2 to this chapter).

7. Golding acknowledges Dickens's greatness in Jack I. Biles, *Talk: Conversations with William Golding*, p. 9; and Virginia Tiger, *William Golding: The Dark Fields of Discovery*, p. 202, notes that "the sturdiest literary furniture of his imagination dates from the nineteenth century—Wells, Dickens, Thackeray, and the robust popular tradition of Henry, Ballantyne, and Burroughs." She also (p. 215) points out Trollopeian qualities in *The Pyramid*. The parallels to *Great Expectations*, however, are numerous and pervasive.

8. Donoghue, "The Ordinary Universe," pp. 21, 22.

9. Compare this scene with *The Inheritors*, pp. 200–4, and with *Free Fall*, pp. 20–21.

10. John Bowen, "Bending Over Backwards," *Times Literary Supplement*, p. 608.

11. See James Keating, "Interview with William Golding," Casebook Edition of *Lord of the Flies*, p. 195, Frank Kermode, "The Meaning of It All," *Books and Bookmen*, p. 9, and Biles, *Talk*, pp. 18, 53–58, 75.

Notes

12. Martin Green, "Distaste for the Contemporary," *The Nation*, p. 454.

13. Donoghue, "The Ordinary Universe," p. 21.

8: *Darkness Visible*

1. Virginia Tiger, *William Golding: The Dark Fields of Discovery*, p. 228.

2. John Milton, *Paradise Lost*, ed. Merritt Y. Hughes, Book 1, ll. 61–63, p. 7.

3. Publius Vergilius Maro, *The Aeneid*, trans. Allen Mandelbaum, Book 6, ll. 353–55, P. 141.

4. William Golding, *Darkness Visible* (New York: Farrar, Straus & Giroux, 1979), p. 11; further parenthetical references in the text are taken from this edition.

5. See Golding on homosexuality in Jack I. Biles, *Talk: Conversations with William Golding*, pp. 111–12.

Bibliography

I. PRIMARY SOURCES

1. Poetry, Drama, and Fiction by William Golding

Included here are the first British and American editions of the works listed, as well as useful paperback editions which preserve the original pagination.

Poems. London: Macmillan, 1934; also New York: Macmillan, 1935.
Lord of the Flies. London: Faber & Faber, 1954; also New York: Coward-McCann, 1955, and Casebook Edition, text notes & criticism, edited by James R. Baker and Arthur P. Ziegler, Jr. New York: G. P. Putnam's Sons, 1964.
The Inheritors. London: Faber & Faber, 1955; also New York: Harcourt, Brace & World, 1962, 1963.
Pincher Martin. London: Faber & Faber, 1956; also *The Two Deaths of Christopher Martin.* New York: Harcourt, Brace & World, 1957; and *Pincher Martin.* New York: G. P. Putnam's Sons, 1962.
"Envoy Extraordinary." In *Sometime, Never: Three Tales of Imagination* by William Golding, John Wyndham, and Mervyn Peake. London: Eyre & Spottiswoode, 1956, pp. 11–78; also New York: Ballantine Books, 1962, pp. 3–60.
The Brass Butterfly. London: Faber & Faber, 1958.
Free Fall. London: Faber & Faber, 1959; also New York: Harcourt, Brace & World, 1960, 1962.
"The Anglo-Saxon." *The Queen* 215 (22 December 1959): 27–30.
Miss Pulkinhorn. BBC radio play, 20 April 1960. Unpublished.
"Miss Pulkinhorn." *Encounter* 15 (August 1960): 27–32.
Break My Heart. BBC radio play, 19 March 1961. Unpublished.
The Spire. London: Faber & Faber, 1964; also New York: Harcourt, Brace & World, 1964, 1965.
"Inside a Pyramid." *Esquire* 66 (December 1966): 165–69.
"On the Escarpment." *Kenyon Review* 29 (June 1967): 311–400.
The Pyramid. London: Faber & Faber, 1967; also New York: Harcourt, Brace & World, 1967, 1968.
The Scorpion God. London: Faber & Faber, 1971; also New York: Harcourt, Brace Jovanovich, 1972.
Darkness Visible. New York: Farrar, Straus & Giroux, 1979.

2. Essays and Reviews by William Golding

Several of the following (marked +) are included in *The Hot Gates and Other Occasional Pieces.* London: Faber & Faber, 1965; also New York: Harcourt, Brace & World, 1967.

"The Writer in His Age." *London Magazine* 4 (May 1957): 45–46.
"Pincher Martin." *Radio Times* 138 (21 March 1958): 8.

Bibliography

+ "The Ladder and the Tree." *The Listener* 63 (24 March 1960): 531–33.

"In Retreat." *The Spectator* 204 (25 March 1960): 448–49.

"Raider." *The Spectator* 204 (20 May 1960): 741.

+ "Islands." *The Spectator* 204 (10 June 1960): 844–46.

+ "On the Crest of the Wave." *Times Literary Supplement* (17 June 1960): 387.

+ "Headmasters." *The Spectator* 205 (12 August 1960): 252–53.

+ "In My Ark." *The Spectator* 205 (16 September 1960): 409.

"Man of God." *The Spectator* 205 (7 October 1960): 530.

+ "Billy the Kid." *The Spectator* 205 (25 November 1960): 808, 811.

"Prospect of Eton." *The Spectator* 205 (25 November 1960): 856–57.

"Thin Partitions." *The Spectator* 206 (13 January 1961): 49.

"Rise of Love." *The Spectator* 206 (10 February 1961): 194.

"Androids All." *The Spectator* 206 (24 February 1961): 263–64.

"All or Nothing." *The Spectator* 206 (24 March 1961): 410.

"Before the Beginning." *The Spectator* 206 (26 May 1961): 768.

+ "Astronaut by Gaslight." *The Spectator* 206 (9 June 1961): 841–42.

"It's a Long Way to Oxyrhynchus." *The Spectator* 207 (7 July 1961): 9.

"Party of One: Thinking as a Hobby." *Holiday* 30 (August 1961): 8 ff.

+ "Tolstoy's Mountain." *The Spectator* 207 (8 September 1961): 325–26.

+ "A Touch of Insomnia." *The Spectator* 207 (27 October 1961): 569–71.

+ "The Glass Door." *The Spectator* 207 (24 November 1961): 732–33.

+ "The English Channel." *Holiday* 30 (November 1961): 32 ff.

+ "Body and Soul." *The Spectator* 208 (19 January 1962): 65–66.

"Through the Dutch Waterways." *Holiday* 31 (January 1962): 58 ff.

+ "Shakespeare's Birthplace." *Holiday* 31 (May 1962): 82 ff.

+ "Gradus ad Parnassum." *The Spectator* 209 (7 September 1962): 327–29.

"Surge and Thunder." *The Spectator* 209 (14 September 1962): 370.

+ "Digging for Pictures." *Holiday* 32 (March 1963): 86 ff.

"Party of One: The Best of Luck." *Holiday* 35 (May 1964): 12 ff.

"An Affection for Cathedrals." *Holiday* 36 (December 1965): 35ff.

+ "Egypt and I." *Holiday* 34 (April 1966): 32 ff.

"Wiltshire: The Rural Retreat." *Venture* 7 (September-December 1966): 19–26

"Delphi: The Oracle Revealed." *Holiday* 42 (August 1967): 60.

II. SECONDARY SOURCES

1. Works on Golding

Babb, Howard S. *The Novels of William Golding.* Columbus: The Ohio State University Press. 1970.

Baker, James R. *William Golding, A Critical Study.* New York: St. Martin's Press, 1965.

Biles, Jack I. *Talk: Conversations with William Golding*. New York: Harcourt Brace Jovanovich, Inc., 1970.

Biles, Jack I. and Robert O. Evans, eds. *William Golding: Some Critical Considerations*. Lexington: The University Press of Kentucky, 1979.

Bufkin, Ernest Claude, Jr. "The Novels of William Golding: A Descriptive and Analytical Study." Ph.D. dissertation, Vanderbilt University, 1965.

Dewsnap, Terence. *William Golding's "The Inheritors" and "Free Fall."* Monarch Literature Notes. New York: Monarch Press, 1966.

———. *William Golding's "Lord of the Flies" and "The Inheritors," "Pincher Martin," "Free Fall."* Monarch Literature Notes. New York: Monarch Press, 1964.

———. *William Golding's "Pincher Martin."* Monarch Literature Notes. New York: Monarch Press, 1966.

Dick, Bernard F. *William Golding*. New York: Twayne Publishers, 1967.

Elmen, Paul. *William Golding: A Critical Essay*. Contemporary Writers in Christian Perspective. Grand Rapids, Mich.: Eerdmans, 1967.

Hodson, Leighton. *William Golding*. Edinburgh: Oliver and Boyd, 1969.

Hynes, Samuel. *William Golding*. New York and London: Columbia University Press, 1964.

Jackson, Frederick. *An Outline of "Lord of the Flies."* Toronto: Forum House, 1968.

Kinkead-Weekes, Mark, and Ian Gregor. *William Golding, A Critical Study*. London: Faber & Faber, 1967.

Medcalf, Stephen. *William Golding*. Writers and Their Work, no. 243. London: Longman, 1975.

Moody, Philippa. *A Critical Commentary on William Golding's "Lord of the Flies."* London: Macmillan, 1966.

Oldsey, Bernard S., and Stanley Weintraub. *The Art of William Golding*. New York: Harcourt, Brace & World, 1965.

Pemberton, Clive. *William Golding*. Writers and Their Work, no. 210. London: Longmans, 1969.

Tiger, Virginia. *William Golding: The Dark Fields of Discovery*. London: Calder & Boyars, 1974.

2. General studies with chapters or pages on Golding:

Allen, Walter. *Tradition and Dream*. Harmondsworth: Penguin, 1965.

Amis, Kingsley. *New Maps of Hell*. London: Gollancz, 1961.

Broes, Arthur T. *Lectures on Modern Novelists*. Pittsburgh: Carnegie Series in English, no. 7, 1963.

Burgess, Anthony. *The Novel Today*. London: Longmans, 1963.

———. *The Novel Now*. London: Faber & Faber, 1967.

Cox, C. B. *The Free Spirit*. London: Oxford University Press, 1963.

Fairman, Marion A. *Biblical Patterns in Modern Literature*. Cleveland: Dillon/Liederbach, 1972.

Bibliography

Faulkner, Peter. *Humanism in the English Novel*. London: Elek/Pemberton, 1975.

Friedman, Norman. *Form and Meaning in Fiction*. Athens: University of Georgia Press, 1975.

Gindin, James. *Harvest of a Quiet Eye: The Novel of Compassion*. Bloomington: Indiana University Press, 1971.

———. *Postwar British Fiction*. Berkeley: University of California Press, 1962.

Halliday, M. A. K. "Linguistic Function and Literary Style: An Inquiry into the Language of William Golding's *The Inheritors*." *Literary Style: A Symposium*, Seymour Chatman, ed. London: Oxford University Press, 1971.

Josipovici, Gabriel. *The World and the Book: A Study of Modern Fiction*. Stanford: Stanford University Press; London: Macmillan, 1971.

Karl, Frederick. *A Reader's Guide to the Contemporary English Novel*. New York: Noonday Press, 1962.

Kennard, Jean E. *Number and Nightmare: Forms of Fantasy in Contemporary Fiction*. Hamden, Conn.: Archon Books, 1975.

Kermode, Frank. *Puzzles and Epiphanies*. London: Routledge, 1962.

Mueller, William R. *Celebration of Life: Studies in Modern Fiction*. New York: Sheed and Ward, 1972.

Rexroth, Kenneth. *With Eye and Ear*. New York: Herder, 1970.

Richter, David H. *Fable's End: Completeness and Closure in Rhetorical Fiction*. Chicago: University of Chicago Press, 1974.

Riley, Carolyn, ed. *Contemporary Literary Criticism*. Vols. 1,3. Detroit: Gale, 1973, 1975.

Riley, Carolyn, and Barbara Harte, eds. *Contemporary Literary Criticism*. Vol. 2. Detroit: Gale, 1974.

Robson, W. W. *Modern English Literature*. London: Oxford University Press, 1970.

Rodway, Allan. *The Truths of Fiction*. New York: Schocken Books, 1971.

Smith, Eric. *Some Versions of the Fall*. London: Croom Helm; Pittsburgh: University of Pittsburgh Press, 1973.

Swinden, Patrick. *Unofficial Selves: Character in the Novel from Dickens to the Present Day*. New York: Barnes & Noble, 1973.

Vinson, James, ed. *Contemporary Novelists*. New York: St. Martin's Press, 1972.

West, Paul. *The Modern Novel*. London: Hutchinson, 1963.

3. Articles on Golding

Articles marked (B) may be found in Baker and Ziegler's Casebook Edition of *Lord of the Flies*; those marked (N) may be found in William Nelson, *William Golding's "Lord of the Flies," A Source Book*. New York: The Odyssey Press, 1963. I have indicated particularly useful articles by an asterisk (*).

Of Earth and Darkness

Aarseth, Inger. "Golding's Journey to Hell: An Examination of Pre-figurations and Archetypal Pattern in *Free Fall.*" *English Studies* 56 (August 1975).

Aldridge, John W. "William Golding." *New York Times Book Review* 7 (10 December 1961): 56–57.

Ali, Nasood Amjad. "*The Inheritors*: An Experiment in Technique." *Venture* 5 (April 1969): 123–30.

(N) Allen, Walter. "New Novels." *New Statesman & Nation* 48 (25 September 1954): 370.

Babb, Howard. "On the Ending of *Pincher Martin.*" *Essays in Criticism* 14:1 (January 1964): 106–8.

Biles, Jack I. "An Interview in London with Angus Wilson." *Studies in the Novel* 2 (Spring 1970): 76–87.

———. "Literary Sources and William Golding." *South Atlantic Bulletin* 37 (May 1972): 29–36.

*Biles, Jack I., and Carl R. Kropf. "The Cleft Rock of Conversion: *Robinson Crusoe* and *Pincher Martin.*" *A William Golding Miscellany.* Studies in the Literary Imagination 2:2 (October 1969): 17–43.

Blake, Ian. "*Pincher Martin:* William Golding and 'Taffrail.'" *Notes and Queries* (August 1962): 309–10.

(N) Bowen, John. "One Man's Meat, The Idea of Individual Responsibility." *Times Literary Supplement* (7 August 1959): xii–xiii.

*(N) ———. "Bending Over Backwards." *Times Literary Supplement* (23 October 1959): 608.

Braybrooke, N. "Return of Pincher Martin." *Commonweal* 89 (25 October 1969): 115 ff.

*Bufkin, E. C. "*Pincher Martin:* William Golding's Morality Play." *A William Golding Miscellany.* Studies in the Literary Imagination 2:2 (October 1969): 5–16.

Byatt, A. S. "Of Things I Sing." *New Statesman* 73 (2 June 1967): 481.

(N) Colby, Vineta. "William Golding." *Wilson Library Bulletin* 37 (February 1963): 505.

*(B) Coskren, Thomas M. "Is Golding Calvinistic?" *America* 109 (6 July 1963): 18–20.

(N) Cox, C. B. "*Lord of the Flies.*" *Critical Quarterly* 2(1960): 112–17.

Crane, John Kenny. "Crossing the Bar Twice: Post-Mortem Consciousness in Bierce, Hemingway, and Golding." *Studies in Short Fiction* 6 (Summer 1969): 361–76.

Crompton, D. W. "The Spire." *Critical Quarterly* 9 (Spring 1967): 63–79.

Davies, Cecil W. "The Novels Foreshadowed: Some Recurring Themes in Early Poems by William Golding." *English* 17 (Autumn 1968): 86–89.

Davis, Douglas M. "Golding, The Optimist, Belies His Somber Pictures and Fiction." *National Observer* (17 September 1962): 17.

*———. "Conversation with Golding." *New Republic* 148 (4 May 1963): 28–30.

Bibliography

Delbaere-Garant, Jeanne. "The Evil Plant in William Golding's *The Spire*." *Revue des Langues Vivantes* 35(1969): 623–31.

———. "From the Cellar to the Rock: A Recurrent Pattern in William Golding's Novels." *Modern Fiction Studies* 17 (Winter 1971–1972): 501–12.

———. "Time as a Structural Device in Golding's *Free Fall*." *English Studies* 57(August 1976): 353–65.

———. "William Golding's Pincher Martin." *English Studies* 51 (December 1970): 538–44.

*Dick, Bernard F. "'The Novelist Is a Displaced Person': An Interview with William Golding." *College English* 26 (March 1965): 480–82.

———. "The Pyramid: Mr. Golding's 'New' Novel." *A William Golding Miscellany*. Studies in the Literary Imagination 2:1 (October 1969): 83–95.

*Donoghue, Denis. "The Ordinary Universe." *The New York Review of Books* 9 (7 December 1967): 21–23.

"Down to Earth." *Times Literary Supplement* (1 June 1967): 481.

Drew, Philip. "Second Reading." *Cambridge Review* 78 (1956): 78–84.

Egan, John M. "Golding's View of Man." *America* 108 (16 January 1963): 140–41.

*(B) Epstein, E. L. "Notes on *Lord of the Flies*." *Lord of the Flies*. New York: Capricorn Books, 1959: 249–55.

(B) Forster, E. M. "Introduction." *Lord of the Flies*. New York: Coward-McCann, 1962: ix–xii.

Fox, Dorothy. "William Golding's Microcosms of Evil." *Innisfree* 1(1974): 30–37.

*(N) Freedman, Ralph. "The New Realism: The Fancy of William Golding." *Perspective* 10(1958): 118–28.

(N) Fuller, Edmund. "Behind the Vogue, a Rigorous Understanding." *New York Herald Tribune Weekly Book Review* 39 (4 November 1962): 3.

*Furbank, P. N. "Golding's *Spire*." *Encounter* 22 (May 1964): 59–61.

(N) Grande, Luke M. "The Appeal of Golding." *Commonweal* 17 (25 January 1963): 457–59.

*(N) Green, Martin. "Distaste for the Contemporary." *Nation* 190 (21 May 1960): 451–54.

*(N) Green, Peter. "The World of William Golding." *Review of English Literature* 1:2 (1960): 62–72.

*(B) Gregor, Ian, and Mark Kinkead-Weekes. "Introduction." *Lord of the Flies*. London: Faber & Faber School Editions, 1962: i–xii.

*(N)———. "The Strange Case of Mr. Golding and His Critics." *The Twentieth Century* 167 (February 1960): 115–25.

(N) Halle, Louis J. "Small Savages." *Saturday Review* 38 (15 October 1955): 16.

Hannon, Leslie. "William Golding: Spokesman for Youth." *Cavalier* 13(December 1963): 10–12, 92–93.

Harvey, W. J. "The Reviewing of Contemporary Fiction." *Essays in Criticism* 8(April 1958): 182–87.

(N) Hewitt, Douglas. "New Novels." *The Manchester Guardian* 71 (28 September 1954): 4.

Hough, Graham. "Fables After The Fall." *Saturday Review* 48 (31 July 1965): 17–18.

Hurt, J. R. "Grendel's Point of View: *Beowulf* and William Golding." *Modern Fiction Studies* 13(Summer 1967): 264–65.

(N) Hynes, Samuel. "Novels of a Religious Man." *Commonweal* 71 (18 March 1960): 673–75.

Irwin, Joseph J. "The Serpent Coiled Within." *Motive* 23 (May 1963): 1–5.

Johnston, Arnold. "Innovation and Rediscovery in Golding's *The Pyramid*." *Critique: Studies in Modern Fiction* 14 (1972): 97–112.

(N) Kearns, Francis E. "Salinger and Golding: Conflict on the Campus." *America* 108 (26 January 1963): 136–39.

(N)———, and Luke M. Grande. "An Exchange of Views." *Commonweal* 77 (22 February 1963): 569–71.

(B) Keating, James, and William Golding. "The Purdue Interview." *Lord of the Flies*, edited by Baker and Ziegler (see above).

*(N) Kermode, Frank. "Coral Islands." *The Spectator* 201 (22 August 1958): 257.

*(B)———, and William Golding. "The Meaning of It All." *Books and Bookmen* 5 (October 1959): 9–10.

*(N) (B)———. "The Novels of William Golding." *International Literary Annual* 3 (1961): 11–29.

*———. "The Case for William Golding." *The New York Review of Books* 11(30 April 1964): 3–4.

LaChance, Paul R. "*Pincher Martin*: The Essential Dilemma of Modern Man." *Cithara* 8 (May 1969): 55–60.

Lederer, R., and P. H. Beattie. "*African Genesis* and *Lord of the Flies*: Two Studies of the Beastie Within." *English Journal* 58 (December 1969): 1316–21.

Leed, Jacob R. "*Lord of the Flies*." *Dimension* supplement to *Daily Northwestern* (January 1963): 7–11.

Levitt, L. "Trust the Tale: A Second Reading of *Lord of the Flies*." *English Journal* 58 (April 1969): 521–22.

Lewis, R. W. B. "Free Fall." *New York Herald Tribune Weekly Book Review* (14 February 1960):5.

Lodge, David. "The Novelist at the Crossroads." *Critical Quarterly* 11(Summer 1969): 105–32.

———. "William Golding." *Spectator* (10 April 1964): 489–90.

(N) (B) "Lord of the Campus." *Time* 79 (22 June 1962): 64.

"Lord of the Flies." *America* 109 (5 October 1963): 398.

*Maclure, Millar. "William Golding's Survival Stories." *Tamarack Review* 4(Summer 1957): 60–67.

*———. "Allegories of Innocence." *Dalhousie Review* 40 (Summer 1960): 144–56.

MacShane, Frank. "The Novels of William Golding." *Dalhousie Review* 40 (Summer 1962): 171–83.

Bibliography

Marcus, Steven. "The Novel Again." *Partisan Review* 29 (Spring 1962): 179–84.

Martin, J. "Symbol Hunting Golding's *Lord of the Flies.*" *English Journal* 58(March 1969): 408–13.

Mayne, Richard. "*Pincher Martin.*" *New Statesman & Nation* 52 (27 October 1956): 524.

(B) Mueller, William R. "An Old Story Well Told." *Christian Century* 80 (2 October 1963): 1203–06.

*(N) Niemeyer, Carl. "The Coral Island Revisited." *College English* 22 (1960): 241–45.

Nordell, Roderick. "Book Report." *Christian Science Monitor* (27 December 1962): 9.

Nossen, Evon. "The Beast-Man Theme in the Work of William Golding." *Ball State University Forum* 9 (1968): 60–69.

*Oldsey, Bernard, and Stanley Weintraub. "*Lord of the Flies*: Beelzebub Revisited." *College English* 25 (November 1963): 90–99.

*(N) (B) Peter, John. "The Fables of William Golding." *Kenyon Review* 19 (1957): 577–92.

Plimpton, George. "Without the Evil to Endure." *New York Times Book Review* (29 July 1962): 4.

Podhoretz, Norman. "A Look at Life." *New Yorker* 33 (21 September 1957): 189–90.

(N) Pritchett, V. S. "Secret Parables." *New Statesman* 61 (2 August 1958): 146–47.

———. "God's Folly." *New Statesman* 67 (10 April 1964): 562–63.

*Quinn, Michael. "An Unheroic Hero: William Golding's 'Pincher Martin.'" *Critical Quarterly* 4(Autumn 1962): 247–56.

Renault, Mary. "Free Fall." *Saturday Review* 43 (19 March 1960):21.

*Roper, D. "Allegory and Novel in Golding's *The Spire.*" *Wisconsin Studies in Contemporary Literature* 8 (Winter 1967): 19–30.

*(B) (N) Rosenfield, Claire. "Men of a Smaller Growth: A Psychological Analysis of William Golding's *Lord of the Flies.*" *Literature and Psychology* 11 (Autumn 1961): 83–101.

Ryan, J. S. "The Two Pincher Martins: From Survival Adventure to Golding's Myth of Dying." *English Studies* 55 (1974): 140–51.

Sasso, Laurence J., Jr. "A Note on the Dwarf in *Pincher Martin.*" *Massachusetts Studies in English* 1(1968): 66–68.

*Seymour-Smith, Martin. "Golding's Pyramid." *Spectator* 243 (30 June 1967): 768–69.

*Skilton, David. "Golding's *The Spire.*" *A William Golding Miscellany.* Studies in the Literary Imagination 2:2 (October 1969): 45–56.

Smith, P. D. "Hear the Preacher." *New Statesman* 58 (24 October 1959): 550–51.

*(B) Spangler, D. R. "Simon." *Lord of the Flies*, Casebook Edition.

Spitz, David. "Power and Authority: An Interpretation of Golding's *Lord of the Flies.*" *Antioch Review* 30 (Spring 1970): 21–33.

(N) Stern, James. "English Schoolboys in the Jungle." *New York Times* (23 October 1955): 23.

Sternlicht, S. "Songs of Innocence and Songs of Experience in *Lord of the Flies*." *Midwest Quarterly* 9(July 1968): 383–90.

——. "Two Views of the Builder in Graham Greene's *A Burnt-Out Case* and William Golding's *The Spire*." *Calcutta Review* (March 1970): 401–4.

Stinson, John J. "Trying to Exorcise the Beast: The Grotesque in the Fiction of William Golding." *Cithara* 11 (1971): 3–30.

Sullivan, Walter. "The Long Chronicle of Guilt: William Golding's *The Spire*." *Hollins Critic* 1 (June 1964): 1–12.

*Sutherland, Raymond Carter. Mediaeval Elements in *The Spire*." *A William Golding Miscellany*. Studies in the Literary Imagination 2:2 (October 1969): 57–65.

*Talon, H. "Irony in *Lord of the Flies*." *Essays in Criticism* 18(July 1968): 296–309.

Thomson, George H. "The Real World of William Golding." *Alphabet* 9(November 1964): 26–33.

——. "William Golding: Between God-Darkness and God-Light." *Cresset* (June 1969):8–12.

Townsend, R. C. "*Lord of the Flies*: Fool's Gold?" *Journal of General Education* 16 (July 1964): 153–60.

Trilling, Lionel. "*Lord of the Flies*." *The Midcentury* 45 (October 1962):10.

*Wain, John. "Lord of the Agonies." *Aspect* 3 (April 1963):56–67.

*Walker, Marshall. "William Golding: From Paradigm to Pyramid." *A William Golding Miscellany*. Studies in the Literary Imagination 2:2 (October 1969): 67–82.

*(N) Walters, Margaret. "Two Fabulists: Golding and Camus." *Melbourne Critical Review* 4 (1961):18–29.

*Webster, Owen. "Living with Chaos." *Books and Art* (March 1958):15–16.

White, Robert J. "Butterfly and Beast in *Lord of the Flies*." *Modern Fiction Studies* 10 (Summer 1964): 163–70.

Whitehead, John. "A Conducted Tour to the Pyramid." *London Magazine* 7 (June 1967): 100–4.

Whitehead, Lee M. "Moment Out of Time: Golding's *Pincher Martin*." *Contemporary Literature* 12 (Winter 1971): 18–41.

(N) Wickenden, Dan. "First Idyll, Then Nightmare." *New York Herald Tribune Weekly Book Review* 32 (23 October 1955): 6.

(N) Young, Wayland. "Letter from London." *Kenyon Review* 19 (Summer 1957): 477–82.

4. Corollary readings

Alighieri, Dante. *The Inferno*. Translated by John Ciardi. New York: New American Library, 1960.

——. *The New Life (La Vita Nuova)*. Translated by Dante Gabriel Rossetti. London, 1889.

Ballantyne, R. M. *The Coral Island*. London and Glasgow: Collins, 1954.

Bibliography

Camus, Albert. *The Fall*. Translated by Justin O'Brien. New York: Knopf, 1956.

Defoe, Daniel. *Robinson Crusoe*. New York: Washington Square Press, 1963.

Dickens, Charles. *Great Expectations*. New York: Bobbs-Merrill, 1964.

Dodds, E. R. *Euripides' Bacchae*. Second Edition. Oxford: Clarendon Press, 1960.

Ford, George H. *Double Measure: A Study of the Novels and Stories of D. H. Lawrence*. New York: Holt, Rinehart and Winston, 1965.

Frazer, Sir James George. *The New Golden Bough*. Edited by Theodor H. Gaster. New York: Anchor Books, 1961.

Freud, Sigmund. *Totem and Taboo*. Translated by James Strachey. New York: W. W. Norton, 1950.

———. *Civilization and Its Discontents*. Translated by James Strachey. New York: W. W. Norton, 1961.

Hughes, Richard. *A High Wind in Jamaica*. New York: New American Library, 1961.

Joyce, James. *A Portrait of the Artist As A Young Man*. New York: Viking Press, 1964.

Lawrence, D. H. *Sons and Lovers*. New York: Viking Press, 1968.

Maro, Publius Vergilius. *The Aeneid*. Translated by Allen Mandelbaum. Berkeley, Los Angeles, London: The University of California Press, 1971.

Milton, John. *Paradise Lost*. Edited by Merritt Y. Hughes. New York: The Odyssey Press, 1962.

The Battle of Maldon and Other Old English Poems. Translated by Kevin Crossley-Holland. Edited by Bruce Mitchell. New York: St. Martin's Press, 1967.

Wells, H. G. *Outline of History*. Garden City, N.J.: Garden City Publishing Company, 1931.

Williams, Charles. *The Figure of Beatrice, A Study in Dante*. New York: Noonday Press, 1961.

Index

Index

Index

K

Kermode, Frank, 6, 9, 54
King Lear, 42, 43–44
King of Hearts, The, 84, 88, 95
Kinkead-Weekes, Mark (with Ian Gregor), ii, 18–19, 24, 49, 65, 83
Künstlerroman, 50

L

La Vita Nuova, 59, 60, 63
"Ladder and Tree, The," 85
Lawrence, D. H., 51, 60, 64
Liar, the, 98
Liku, 22, 28, 29, 30, 31, 32
Lok, 2, 22, 23, 24, 25, 27, 28, 29, 30–32, 33, 68, 74, 100
Lord of the Flies, i–iv *passim*, 1, 4, 5, 6, 7, 8–19, 21, 24, 26, 30, 33, 34, 35, 36, 37, 38, 46, 48, 52, 55, 56, 68, 71, 73, 81
Lord of the Flies, 12–13. *See also Ba'al zevuv*; Beelzebub
Lovell, Mary, 46, 58

M

Ma, 56, 57, 58, 64
Magwitch, 93, 94
Main Street, 95
Mal, 22, 25, 26, 29
Marlan, 31, 33
Marlborough, 85
Marlborough Grammar School, 1
Martin, Christopher, iii, 15, 36–49, 53, 58, 61, 68, 74, 86, 100, 107
Marx, Karl, 38
Mason, Rachel, 73, 76
Mason, Roger, 15, 72, 73, 75, 76, 78, 79
Masterman, Fido, 105, 107
Merridew, Jack, 9, 11, 12, 13, 14, 16, 41, 100, 107
Milton, John, 43, 98
Minnie, 57, 62
Miriam, 60
Miss Havisham, 94
Mrs. Joe, 93
"Mr. Pope," 3
Mr. Wopsle, 93
Morel, Paul, 51, 60, 64
Moses, 61, 62, 64

Mountjoy, Sammy, iii, 15, 50, 51–66, 68, 69, 70, 78, 79, 80, 86, 87, 90–91, 95, 96, 100, 110
Myth: as literary mode, 6, 7, 18, 19, 30, 31, 34, 42, 44, 45, 49, 83. *See also* Golding as "myth-maker"

N

Neanderthal man, 21–24 *passim*, 27, 28, 31, 33
"New one," the, 22, 29, 30, 32, 34
New Testament, 60, 102
Niemeyer, Carl, 9
Nil, 22, 29

O

Oa, 22, 23, 32
"Occurrence at Owl-Creek Bridge, An," 37, 44
Oldsey, Bernard S. (with Stanley Weintraub), ii, 4, 21, 44
Old Testament, 60, 102
Old Woman, the, 22, 28, 29–30
Oliver, 15, 83–93, 96
Oliver's father, 85, 87, 89
"On the Escarpment," 83
Original Sin, ii, 21, 22, 27, 34
Orlick, 94
Outline of History, The, iii, 21, 31, 81
Oxford University, 2, 3, 4, 5, 84, 85, 86

P

Pangall, Goody, 70, 71, 73, 75–76, 77
Pangall, 71, 73, 76, 81
Papal Visitor, 77
Paradise Hill, 54, 57, 62
Paradise Lost, 43
Paradiso, 60, 62–63
Pedigree, Sebastian, 100, 101, 106, 108, 109
Pete, 39, 40, 41, 45
Peter, John, 5–6, 18, 49, 65, 83
Peterkin, 9
Piggy, 11–14 *passim*, 16, 17, 19, 41
Pig-killing, 12–13, 48, 107

Index

Index